And God Said, "No!"

T. J. Padgett
with Jordan Fennell

TRILOGY CHRISTIAN PUBLISHERS
TUSTIN, CA

TRILOGY

Trilogy Christian Publishers
A Wholly Owned Subsidiary of Trinity Broadcasting Network
2442 Michelle Drive
Tustin, CA 92780

And God Said, "No!"
Trilogy Christian Publishers A Wholly Owned Subsidiary of Trinity Broadcasting
Copyright © 2023 by T. J. Padgett

Scripture quotations marked KJV are taken from the King James Version of the Bible. Public domain.

No part of this book may be reproduced, stored in a retrieval system, or transmitted by any means without written permission from the author. All rights reserved. Printed in the USA.

Rights Department, 2442 Michelle Drive, Tustin, CA 92780.

Trilogy Christian Publishing/TBN and colophon are trademarks of Trinity Broadcasting Network.

Cover design by: __

For information about special discounts for bulk purchases, please contact Trilogy Christian Publishing.

Trilogy Disclaimer: The views and content expressed in this book are those of the author and may not necessarily reflect the views and doctrine of Trilogy Christian Publishing or the Trinity Broadcasting Network.

Manufactured in the United States of America

10 9 8 7 6 5 4 3 2 1

Library of Congress Cataloging-in-Publication Data is available.

ISBN: 979-8-88738-597-6

E-ISBN: 979-8-88738-598-3 (e-book)

Contents

Foreword v

Chapter 1 1

Chapter 2 22

Chapter 3 33

Chapter 4 60

Chapter 5 87

Chapter 6 103

Chapter 7 126

Chapter 8 146

Chapter 9 172

Epilogue 182

Foreword

I've been blessed.

A lot of people say that today. It has become a common phrase, and some people repeat it over and over until it does not really mean anything. But I mean it. When I look at my life, I know that God has truly blessed me. I turned eighty years old in May of 2022, and I still get around better than most people in their thirties. In fact, the only medicine I take is a water pill and a few vitamins. I can still lift small weights and walk three and a half miles on my treadmill six days a week without getting too winded. As they say, if you do not have your health, you do not have much of anything. The Lord has blessed me to still be in good health even at my age, and I thank Him for that. When I was sixty years old, I decided to clear out the trees around my home and dig a pond. I hired a couple of young men in their late teens and early twenties to help me, and they could not believe how hard and fast I worked. When we were taking a break one day, one of them even asked me, "How old did you say you were?"

Speaking of that pond, I can look out of my window and see the ducks playing in it. The pond wraps around the back of my home, and I can see the tree line beyond the pond and the swimming pool out back. Nowadays, I live the life I have always wanted, in a peaceful spot out in the country in Southeast Georgia. My home might be considered large and fancy by some, but I do not see it that way. The acres of land I own surrounding my home, my vehicles—none of that is for me to brag about. As far as I'm concerned, none of these things are truly mine. They are things God has blessed me with. When it comes down to it, He owns it all, and I give all the glory to Him.

But what I thank God for most is something beyond any material possession. What matters most is that my wife, Deloris, is here with me. Through sixty years of marriage, Deloris has been a steadfast woman of God, and without her, I would never have gotten to where I am today. We have had our difficulties like any husband and wife, but I know the Lord sent her to me. She was part of His plan for my life, I was part of His plan for her life, and I thank Him for that most precious gift. Her advice, wisdom, and support have kept me going through so many dark times in my life, and I strive to do the same for her because she is worth it and then some. We have always been a team, and the notion of divorce never once crossed our minds. I have been blessed with children, grandchildren, and an entire extended family that I love dearly. It seems like Satan has always been after my family and me, but God has always protected us and spared us, just like He protected Job. Throughout this book, you will see plenty of times when it looked like Satan had us beaten, but God always prevailed.

God has blessed me in my work life and my business life, just as He said He would many years ago. I am living proof that

He keeps His promises. This book is going to show you, in detail, how God turned me from a man who was just getting by into a man who now owns an extraordinarily successful business. It was not easy, and it did not happen overnight, but He helped me every step of the way. He was always there guiding me in my endeavors, and I have never forgotten to give back to Him, although I will never be able to fully repay Him.

Because of everything He has done for me, I make it a priority to spend time with Him. Every day I wake up early, shower, shave, and go into my prayer closet. It is not a large room, and it is not decorated with anything fancy, but to me, it is the most important room in my home because I have made it a special place to commune with God. It is His very own room in my home, and He is always welcome. I make sure to spend scheduled time with Him in the mornings and before I go to bed at night. I talk to Him throughout the day because I have worked hard to build a deep, personal relationship with Him. Sometimes His presence is so strong that I must turn around and look because it feels like He is standing in the room with me! I talk to Him like a friend, telling Him about my day, thoughts, troubles, and questions, but most of all, I ask Him what He wants of me and how I can be a better servant for Him.

But it was not always this way.

Before God called me into His service, I was not always the man I should have been. I have made more than my share of mistakes, and I thank Him for choosing to set me on this new path.

The purpose of this book is not to show off any success I have achieved. As I said earlier, all the good things in my life have come to me by God's hands, and I would like for you to view any success of mine that I talk about in this book as an example of the power of God working in the life of an ordinary man. I am no one special, but God decided to call me to His service and to bless my life and the lives of my loved ones. There was a time when I did not listen to Him. There were times when I was not the man of God I am today. When I talk about those times, I do not want you to follow those poor examples. Instead, I want to use my faults and failings to show you how God changed me from that man into the man I am today. It is also because I want to be honest with you about who I am, where I have been, where I am now, and what I am headed toward in the service of my King.

No, the purpose of this book is not for me to show off. God has blessed me beyond anything I will ever deserve, and I want no glory for it since He is the only one who deserves any recognition. The real purpose of this book is to show you how good God has been to me. He has done extraordinary things in my life, and it gives me a lot of pleasure to share these stories with others. When I think about how good He has been to me, I cannot help myself. I want to tell the entire world what He's done for me. I want you to see how the Lord can work in the life of someone as ordinary and undeserving as me. He changed my life for the better in every way. His love is unconditional and infinite, even when we do not deserve it. Even when we stray from Him, He welcomes us back. You will find plenty of examples of His love and His goodness in the pages of this book. There are times when you will read some things that might seem unbelievable, but I assure you that everything happened the way I put it down in this book. Some of the names and locations have been changed to protect the identities of certain people. Other than that, everything you are about to read is absolutely true.

Before we get started with the story, I want to talk to you directly. First, I want to thank you for taking the time to read this book. If you are already a believer and have given your life to Christ, it is my wish that this book strengthens your faith and devotion to the Creator of all things. If you are not a believer, I cannot change your mind. God Himself will not do that for you since, through His eternal love and mercy, He blessed us with free will. But as you read about the miracles He has worked in my life and the blessings He has bestowed on me, I hope you consider what He can do for you. The choice is yours to make, but it is my wish that you give your heart to Christ as I have so that you may have "a life more abundant and free," just as it tells us in the Scriptures. Believe me when I tell you, it is a life that is much better than anything I could have ever imagined. What He has done for me, He can certainly do for you. I am no prophet, and I am no saint; however, He saw fit to bless me and use me for His will just the same. I will forever be grateful to Him for that. If you only trust in Him, the Father will do anything in the world you believe He can do. He has already done the work. He suffered for us, and He saved us. All He asks is that you believe in Him, and you will be saved. Trust in Him, and He will see you through even the worst times. He will never let you down. I have seen the truth of this in my life, and I am sure this can be the case in your life and the lives of your loved ones.

Regardless of your background, I pray that this simple book will bless you and help you in good times and bad. If this book helps you at all, or if you just enjoy it, I hope you will pass it along to someone else who will enjoy it. I especially hope you will share it with someone who needs to hear of God's love because, even though it might not seem like it sometimes, He is certainly still working in our world today. I am proof of that, and this book is my testimony. May He receive all the glory and honor for it.

Chapter 1

This story starts in a small town in southeast Georgia called Waycross in the year 1942. I was born on Sunday, May 24th, in the same year the United States entered World War II. I will not go into detail about my mother's or my dad's name, but you can call me Tim.

I am sure you have heard of World War II, but I am going to bet that unless you are from Southeast Georgia, you have never heard of Waycross. Let me put it this way: when they took the census two years before I was born, Waycross had a population of just a little over sixteen thousand. That is not a whole lot of people. Most of those people were farmers, people who worked for the farmers, shop owners, or folks who were involved in the timber industry, which was really booming during those years. The biggest tourist draws—even today—is the Okefenokee Swamp, where you can get about as close to an alligator as you would ever want to be. That is, if the mosquitos do not carry you off first. Even today, Waycross has not changed all that much, and I am glad of that. You can take a drive around town and still see some of the old churches, hotels, and buildings from back in those days and even before. It is a place that honors its history. Speaking of which, Waycross even erected what we call the "Wall of Faces" in town to remember the veterans of World War II. It is a town that knows where it comes from and where it is headed.

Unless you are my age, and especially if you do not come from where I am from, it might be difficult for you to understand just how tough things were back then for most people. The big corporations and office jobs had not even thought about coming into little Waycross, Georgia. They still have not, really. There are plenty of big employers there today, but there just was not much opportunity in the 1940s and 1950s. The war made life that much harder since the government made everybody ration necessities like flour and such for the war effort.

In the middle of all that, I was fortunate to have been born into a family that ran a general store in town. We were not well-off by any means, but we were not scrounging around looking for two nickels to scrape together, either. At a time when some people were still using outhouses and pumping water by hand, we had running water and electricity in our home.

Like many men of his generation, my dad joined the Navy and left for World War II. As it turned out, he left to fight the Germans, Italians, and Japanese the same year I was born. Looking back on it now, it is interesting that I was born in the middle of a war that has gone down in history for its association with the Holocaust. Many years later, I would make it my duty to help the Jewish people in any way I could, but as a little kid, I had no idea what the future would hold. But God did. He had a plan for me, even back then.

My dad was not a big man. He did not cut an imposing figure, but he was wiry and tough. According to those who knew him even before the war, he was a little rough around the edges, with a mean streak that could show up at any moment. A lot of men were that way back in those days, though, because life was hard, and you had to be tough just to get by. But when I compare what people had to say about him before the war with the man I knew growing up, there is an enormous difference. I am no psychiatrist, but the war changed him, and not at all for the better. It was what they would call PTSD today, or maybe he'd always had some kind of darkness in his heart that the horrors of war brought to the surface. I do not know. It is not my place to judge him. Only his Creator can do that. All I can do is tell the story, even the parts that are hard to hear and even harder to tell. I loved my dad, but even as a child, I could tell something was wrong. None of us knew that whatever he had experienced over there had planted a ticking time bomb in his mind. One day it would go off, and none of us would ever be the same. But I will leave that for later.

My mother, on the other hand, was a wonderful woman in about every way you could imagine. I have five sisters: Joyce, Barbara, Susan, Debbie, and Stephanie. I was the oldest and the only boy, so Mama and I were close, the way a son and his mother are close, or the way a daughter will often be close to her dad. That is a special bond that I believe comes from the Maker Himself, and I am thankful to Him for blessing me with the mother He gave me. This book is all about how He has blessed me, and my mother really was my first blessing. Not everyone can say they had that kind of mother, but I surely did. Even all these years later, I can honestly say she was my best friend, not just my parent. She was a petite woman, quiet and reserved. She was also a God-fearing woman who kept away from the vices of the world that can drag a person down, and I am glad of that. Mama was a fitting example of what it means to be a good person, and she showed me that example through her own words and actions, not by nagging and controlling me. Not a day went by that I ever had to question her love for me or my siblings.

When I was little, I never wanted to be away from her. I attended the Quarterman Street School from first grade up until seventh grade, and on the first day of school in the first grade, Mama took me to school in her car, even though we only lived three blocks away. I was six years old at the time, and I had never really been away from her for awfully long. So, when Mama left me at the school, and I realized she was not going to be there with me all day, it made perfect sense for me to cut and run. I headed out of that school like my life depended on it and beat her back home on foot! That began my lengthy battle with school, which would come to a head in the twelfth grade, but I'll get to that in a minute.

Neither of my parents attended church regularly, but my grandmother on my mother's side of the family made it a point to take us to the Church of the Nazarene. I still remember that old church. It looked like many churches of its kind back in those days, with the pews, the carpets, the altar, and stained-glass windows. It was not extravagant, and it certainly did not have the atmosphere of the megachurches that came along years later, but even as a child, I could feel something special there. As it says in Matthew 18:20 (KJV), "Where two or three are gathered together in my name, there am I in the midst of them." That was certainly the case at the Church of the Nazarene. There is no doubt in my mind that the Father was in our midst. I could not quite put a name to it because it was just a feeling. It was a good feeling—like I belonged and that everything would be okay, one way or another. Looking back, that is probably the first time I felt the holy presence of my Lord and Savior. My home life might not have been the kind of stuff they wrote fairy tales about years and years ago, but I knew there was something important within the walls of that church. Being in the presence of God at such an early age was a blessing to me because it was like I met Him there. I get something much like that feeling now sometimes when I am around the house or in my prayer closet, except now it is much stronger, much more intense, and much more fulfilling. I have grown so much in Christ over the years, but He was still there for me when I was just a child and later when I was not exactly living the way He wanted me to. That is true love. He has never deserted me. How many times in your life has someone left you when the going got tough, or how many times have you left someone else? If it has not happened to you, just keep living. Everybody goes through it in one way or another, but God never leaves. You can run from Him, you can renounce Him, and live in the ways of the world, but He is still there. He will always welcome you back into His heart every single time, and I felt that for the first time there at Grandmother's church. I am still grateful to Almighty God for allowing me to have such a God-fearing grandmother whose faith in her Savior was plain to see to everyone she knew.

My parents may not have been in the pew every time the church doors were open, but one of the things they taught me was the value of hard work. That is something I have never forgotten, and it is something that has helped me every day of my life. Even though we owned the general store, we all helped to make sure things ran smoothly. We knew we could not just kick back and let the money roll in because if we did not all do our part, the store could not function. There was always something to do. By the time I was old enough to go to school, I would be at the store soon after the last school bell rang, helping to stock shelves, bag groceries for customers, sweep up, and do anything Mama told me to do.

To the outside world, we looked like the ideal, small-town Southern family. We ran a successful store, and my parents appeared to be happily married and did not seem to have any problems between them. My grandmother on my mama's side of the family lived close to us. She was always around, and she was just as nurturing, loving, and encouraging as she could be. But when no one else was looking, our family life could not have been more different.

My dad was not an encouraging parent, to say the least. Some of the earliest conversations I remember having with him revolved around him telling my sisters or me, "You're never going to amount to anything," or "You'll never make a name for yourself." Throughout my childhood, that was his refrain. I would like to think that whatever had changed him during the war made him say those hurtful things to us, but even so, it did not hurt any less. Some people would have been crushed by that, hearing it about every day. But I had my mother, grandmother, and siblings who loved and encouraged me. I knew I was not worthless. Even at six or seven years old, I remember vowing to myself to prove him wrong.

The constant put-downs were one thing, but when he started drinking, the abuse became physical. He favored whiskey but would switch to beer from time to time. It did not matter what he drank, though. Over and over, he saw the need to use his fists to make his point, and he was not choosy when it came to giving us his anger. Even though my mother was no match for him in size or strength, she was usually the one who took the beatings, throwing herself in the way to protect us from him, sacrificing herself over and over, caught between her husband and the children she suddenly had to protect from him. When he chose to single her out, he would make up elaborate stories about how she had been seeing the bread man who made deliveries to the store, and he would produce some wild, paranoid scheme in his mind that just did not make sense to anyone but him. I hated seeing him like that, but even more, I hated what he did when he was caught up in it.

As I grew up, I found myself trying to take my mother's place as the one who provided the sacrifice. I could not stand seeing that happen to her when she had done nothing to deserve it, and I wanted to shield her from those beatings. It played on my mind, even when I was small. I loved my dad, but I was afraid of him most of the time. Whenever he was in the house, there was no telling what would set him off or who he would pick to take it out on.

I will not go into too much detail about the beatings he gave me. If I tried to tell you about every one of them, it would take up a whole book by itself. I remember quite clearly, though, the time he beat me with a rubber hose. It was a thick-walled hose and stiff but limber enough to wrap around an arm, a leg, or your back if swung with enough force. I do not remember why he did it that particular time. No one knew the true motivation behind his madness. I do not even think he could have explained it to me, not that I ever got the chance to question him about his actions. He did not always use something else other than his fists, but I guess hitting me with that hose made sure he did not hurt his hands and did not tire him out as quickly. When he was through, I had deep gashes, welts, and dark, intense bruises all over my arms, legs, and back. I thank God that my mother and grandmother were there for me in the aftermath, as they always were. They might not have been able to stop him, but they were sure going to help me recover as quickly and as completely as possible. I do not recall what they used on my wounds, but it was some kind of salve that reduced the swelling, mended the wounds, and soothed the bruises. I remember them slathering that stuff on all my wounds and how it stung. I had to sleep on my face for three days until my back fully healed.

Taking the beatings myself was one thing, but it enraged me when he hurt my mother. In a way, I was proud when it was me instead of my mother or my sisters. I would rather it have been me than any of them, and it broke my heart to see him hurt my mother. I can still remember one day when he grabbed my mama by the hair and dragged her face down in the gravel outside in front of our house. The pain it set in my heart was something you would think a little kid could not bear, and even all these years later, it hurts me to talk about it. But God has been good to me, and He has seen me through those times. As hard as it was, I eventually reached the point where I could forgive my dad for all he had done to us. God has healed so much of my heart since then, but at the time, it was almost unbearable.

In those days, problems at home were not things you were supposed to talk about, and even if you did, it would have been hard for anybody outside of my family to do anything about it. People dealt with their own problems as best as they could, and we were no different. It might be easy for someone outside of that situation to say, "Why didn't your mother just leave him?" That is easy to say but a lot harder to do, especially with six children to raise. Mama did the best she could, given the circumstances, but I still wish those circumstances had been much different.

Naturally, the problems at home spilled over into my school life. Again, times were different then. I had a tough time concentrating on my studies in school, and I had a tendency to "act out," as they say today, all because of my home life. A few teachers took up time with me and had some idea of what I was dealing with at home, but there wasn't much they could do about it. Today, the Department of Family and Children's Services would have stepped in, but in those days, doing something along those lines would have been seen as simply meddling in the personal lives of the students. One of my teachers even took me aside and told me she wished she could help me, and to this day, I am still thankful for her compassion. She was truly a good person, and to hear her say that helped more than she ever realized.

Most of my teachers, though, were not so understanding. They did not have the time or the patience to deal with me, so I made mostly Cs and Ds throughout school, even though I never failed a grade. All I can say is God was with me through it all, although I never liked school in the first place, and I did not mind letting people know. Things got so bad that I became the whipping boy. Whenever something went wrong, you better believe I was the first one on the list of suspects, even if I was absent that day.

Throughout this time, I began to learn more about Christ and the Bible. One event stays with me. When I was seven years old, my grandmother on my dad's side told me something that shocked me. She said that she would not live to see Christ's return but that I would. She went on to say that she would "take her flight" on a Wednesday at seven o'clock and that I would receive a "double portion" if I was there with her, just like Elijah did with Elisha in 1 Kings and 2 Kings in the Bible. Now, some in the family just shook their heads when she talked like this. They thought she was getting older and becoming senile. Being so young, I had no idea what to make of this. Honestly, I did not dwell on it for many years until the day she died. That part will come later in the story.

She kept taking me to church with her at the Church of the Nazarene. My knowledge of Christ continued to grow, and I clung to this in the face of my problems. As time progressed, I accepted Jesus Christ as my Lord and Savior at the age of thirteen, and to me, it was nothing short of a miracle to know that God saved me. To show my public profession of faith, I was baptized. Grandmother was so happy, and so was I, though I would backslide increasingly over the years until God reached down with His mighty hand and gave me the wake-up call of my life. From then on, I put myself into His service. But that was much, much later.

Now that I think about it, water has had significance in my life. I was baptized in a lake, and I had always liked to be around the water, maybe because I have always loved fishing. Plenty of my friends could go out on their own and go fishing, but my mother never would let me. She said she did not think it was safe since I did not have a lot of experience swimming. This did not make a lot of sense to me, as my parents had built a small, homemade concrete swimming pool in our backyard that my sisters and I would swim in during the summer months. Mothers, though, tend to be that way sometimes. It was because she never learned how to swim herself, or it was her feminine intuition. For whatever reason, she would not budge about me going fishing by myself for the longest time. That was until I experienced the second miracle of my life.

We had taken a trip down to Florida to go to the beach. Back then, those beaches and vacation spots were not so crowded, and you did not have to take out a second mortgage just to go on a trip. We were all there: my mother, my grandmother, my sisters, and one of my sister's friends. I cannot recall her name, but she was the friend of my sister Joyce. My dad was not with us that day since he had chosen to go fishing at Fort Frederica back in Georgia.

I was thirteen, and my sister Joyce was almost twelve at the time. We had been playing around in the water, building sandcastles, drawing in the sand with our fingers and such, just doing what kids usually do at the beach, when, unbeknownst to the rest of us, Joyce's friend bumped into her while they were out playing in the water. They were not out extremely far and were only about waist deep. I want to be clear that my sister's friend meant no harm in doing what she did. They were just horsing around in the water, like all the other kids that day at the beach. But, unlike all the other kids, Joyce went under and found herself in a life-or-death situation. Once she went under, the rip tide caught her and dragged her out into the sea. She came up way out in the water, much further away from the shore compared to where she had gone under. It all happened so fast that none of us realized what was going on until my mother said something. I stopped whatever it was I had been doing and spotted Joyce way out near the end of the jetties, and I could tell something was wrong. She was thrashing in the water and hollering, but her screams were interrupted as her head kept dipping below the surface of the water.

Before long, my mother was yelling for help. She could not swim, but she rushed out into the water, pushing forward until she had to really fight to keep her footing. The lifeguards had spotted Joyce by then. My mom frantically begged the lifeguards for help. What they told us made my heart sink—Joyce was too far out for even the lifeguards to go after her on their own, so they would have to get one of their boats ready. To make matters even worse, they informed us that sharks would be in the water that far from the shore. The lifeguards did their best to stay calm and professional, but I could tell by the tone of their voices that it was a race against time and that it was already too late for my sister. By the time they reached her with the boat, she would be gone.

Looking back, I should not have done what I did. It just did not make sense. I had never been out in the ocean like that, and

I sure did not have any experience swimming for such a long distance, much less with the added pressure of rescuing another person who was scared and thrashing around in the water. But I did not think. I acted.

Mother was already out in the water up to her neck when I hit the water at a dead run. It did not take long before I reached my mother, who was already spitting and sputtering, half-crying and half-choking on salt water. "Go back," I told her. "I can't save you both." She looked at me then, and for a moment, she acted as though she didn't hear me. But she saw the determination in my eyes and heard the seriousness in my voice. Reluctantly, she turned and looked back to the shore, then began struggling back to safety.

I was young then, but that still does not explain what I did. Without any thought about my own safety, I kept pushing through the waves until I finally had to dive in. I had never been out so far that I could not feel the bottom under my feet, but I did not have time to get scared. My sister needed me, and I was the only one that could help her. Well, that is not really true. God helped me that day. The strength it took, the raw endurance, and the lack of fear all came from Him—of that, I am sure. I swam as hard as I could, as if I had done it every day of my life. My mind was so focused on saving my sister that my body figured everything out on its own. If Joyce had not been drowning, there is no way I could have swum that far or that fast. With the help of Almighty God, I finally reached my sister. She was a mess, and rightfully so. She was fighting for her life, and I could tell she did not have long before her fight would be over for good. Once I got close enough, I told her to calm down and that I would get her back to shore. At first, she reached out for me, trying to grab me like a life preserver, but I told her not to touch me. I knew that if she grabbed onto me, she would take us both under. I had to stay calm and levelheaded if either of us was going to make it back to that shore alive. I instructed her to float on her back as best as she could, and I alternated between helping to keep her afloat and gently pushing her back toward the shore. I kept this up for what seemed like forever, but I do not recall getting winded or tired in the least. Once we were back to safety, I saw the lifeguards put their boat in the water. If we had waited for the lifeguards, this would have been a quite different story, and I would be recalling my sister's funeral instead of one of God's miracles in my life.

Once we made it to the shore, my mother wrapped my sister in her arms. She was still crying, but now they were tears of joy. All my fatigue set in just as all the adrenaline in my body subsided, and I felt like I could have slept for a week straight. Thankfully, I never did see any of the sharks that regularly patrolled those waters. They did not bother the beachgoers since the sharks preferred to stay further out where the rip tide agitated the bottom and stirred up things that they would feed on. Years later, I would fish for sharks in those same waters and in places near there. They were not extremely large, but they were big and fierce enough that after I had hooked them, I would have to shoot them in the head before I dragged them into the boat. There is not a doubt in my mind that there were sharks out there as I swam to rescue my sister. There is no telling how many of them saw me or swam right by me on my way to her. But God told them, "No," much like when He saved Daniel in the lion's den. When I think about the way I saved my sister, it was God working through me to accomplish His will that day, but there is a lesson there, too. Other people might give up on you or say they will be there to help but never quite give you the help you need in time, just like the lifeguards would have been too late to save Joyce. The distance is too far. There are too many sharks out there, too many obstacles. People can let you down, but God never will. Even when things look grim, He is always there, determined to save you against all odds. There again, you must want His help, and you must do as He commands. If Joyce had not listened to me, I could not have helped her. In fact, we would have both drowned out there that day. After that, my mother let me go fishing whenever and wherever I wanted since I had proven to her that I could more than take care of myself in the water.

***

To say that things at home and at school were still difficult was an understatement. I attended Waycross High School from the eighth until the tenth grade, and the situation did not get any better at all. One extraordinary thing happened to me during that time, however. When I was fourteen years old, I met a special person by the name of Deloris. She was thirteen at the time. Neither one of us knew it, but she would one day be my wife, the mother of my children, my confidant, and so much more. The Scriptures call a person's spouse their "helpmate," and she would be that and more for me. At the time of this writing, we are closing in on sixty years of marriage together, and having her in my life for all these years has been the biggest blessing of all.

It makes sense that our marriage has lasted this long since we started our relationship based on going to church. In those days, church and school were the only ways teenagers could meet one another and spend any time together unless they snuck out of the house and all of that. Neither her parents nor my parents would have stood for that, so I started going to church with her at the Church of God of Prophecy. We were just kids then. We did not have any money to speak of, so as we kept seeing each other, we were more than content just to be in each other's company. Today, we would have been given some spending money by our parents and gone to the movies, restaurants, and the typical haunts of young people in small towns, such as hanging out at the river, but we did not have those options. Instead, I would go over to her house after church on Sundays. We would simply hold hands, watch some television, and talk. We never had a real first date, and that was all right by us. We did not need much to be happy. Just to be with each other was enough.

Deloris' parents took to me quickly, and rightfully so. Even though they knew I was a little rough around the edges in school, I was always good to Deloris and went out of my way to be respectful toward them. But there was still some friction there. Deloris' dad had known of my dad before the war, and that reputation carried over to me the way it often does in small towns. If there was ever a man that was the opposite of my dad, it was Deloris' dad. He was calm, reserved, soft-spoken, and easygoing. One thing I will always remember about him and his entire family was that they stayed out of other people's business. If you are from a small town or know people who are, you will understand how rare that can be. It was a surprise to me that they did not really want me to see their daughter, but I guess since it directly affected them, they were concerned. Now that I have my own children and grandchildren, I can see where they were coming from, and I do not hold any of that against them. Even though they did not like it, to begin with, I was determined to show that I was the kind of guy who would treat Deloris right and that I wasn't anything like my dad. I must have done a decent job because they allowed me to keep seeing her, and for that, I'm still grateful to them, though her mom and dad passed on years ago.

My family did not have much, but we were not destitute. Deloris' family was not, either, but when we started seeing each other, I noticed she would only wear one or two simple dresses. I did not think much of it since Deloris has never been a flashy person, even back then, but kids can be cruel to one another. It is especially rough on girls when they hit their teenage years. I did not witness this when we first started seeing each other, but as luck would have it, we ended up finally attending the same school together when I left Waycross High to go to Hoboken High from the tenth to the eleventh grade. By then, she was fifteen, and I was sixteen. It was a blessing for me to get to see her every day at school, but I noticed how some of the other girls would tease her about her simple dresses and put her down. She would wear the same pair of shoes, day in and day out, until the nails wore through and stabbed her feet when she walked. There were plenty of people like that in those days because times were hard, and money was tight. I had known grown people like that and never thought any less of them. That is just the way things were for some folks in that area. It bothered me to see them treat her that way, and as much as I wanted to say something about it, it really was not my place. She would not have wanted me to make a scene either, but it did not make a lot of sense to me. In my eyes, she was wonderful and beautiful no matter how she dressed—she did not need a brand-new dress, makeup, and a string of pearls to be pretty. I was glad I got to see her every day at school, and she felt the same way about me. Like I said before, we have always appreciated the little things in life and the things that really matter. God has blessed us tremendously over the years in every way possible, but we've never lost sight of the things that really matter, and we appreciate everything we have, no matter how great or small.

Looking back on that time when we went to school together, I would say life was rather good. The situation at home was not getting any better, but it was not getting any worse, either. All that would be short-lived, though. Deloris went back to Ware County High in the eleventh grade, and I stayed at Hoboken High until the twelfth grade. It was rough for me to be apart from her after seeing her every day like that. But that was the least of my worries because I was about to experience an event that would forever change the course of my life.

Remember when I said I was always suspect number one at school whenever anything went wrong? Well, that did not help matters when I got caught smoking one day during December of my last year of high school. Now, the smoking incident is not what you think. I did not get in trouble just for smoking. I got in trouble for smoking when I was not supposed to. You may not be old enough to remember this, but a long time ago, smoking was allowed in school during specified times. Men twenty years younger than me will tell you that when they were in school, they would even smoke cigarettes with their teachers during school hours—if it was in the designated smoking areas, during the specified smoking times. A lot of schools had what they called smoking pits, which were just big ditches on the school grounds where the teachers and students would throw their cigarette butts. Schools did not have many environmental regulations back then, obviously, and in those years, it was completely acceptable for just about everybody to smoke cigarettes. It was a different time and a different world. So no, I did not get in trouble for smoking—I got in trouble for smoking outside of the designated smoking time. Now, to be fair, I did the crime, and I knew I was going to be punished. I figured it would be something minor since this kind of thing happened all the time. But my reputation as suspect number one had followed me over the years, and when it came time to pick out punishment for me, the principal did not hesitate to pull out the big guns.

There I was, seventeen years old, sitting in his office. He glared across his desk at me. I knew he had a stack of discipline forms and write-up slips he had collected on me, but he did not reach for a new one. Instead, he leaned across his desk and told me to prepare for a paddling. Corporal punishment was common in those days, so it was not unheard of. The only problem was I had spent my entire life either trying not to take a beating from my dad or actively trying to take beatings so my dad would not hurt my mother or my sisters.

What the principal was saying was reasonable, at least by the school's rules, but by that point, I'd had enough. This man was not about to hit me. Nobody had the right to lay a hand on me. I told him plainly that he wasn't going to paddle me. He countered by saying that if I would not submit to the punishment prescribed, then it would be best if I left the school.

Nowadays, that would be a lawsuit since schools have plenty of ways to punish students without jumping to physical violence. At that time, though, those were my only two options. I left school just shy of graduating. There was not much work around Waycross, Georgia, at the time, especially for a seventeen-year-old without a high school diploma. The only path available to me would have been manual labor, working on a farm, getting on with a timber crew, or I could have stayed at home, working in my family's general store.

None of those choices appealed to me. Other than my mother, my sisters, and Deloris, there really was not much keeping me there. In the back of my mind, I kept hearing my dad's voice telling me that I would never amount to anything. For the first time in my life, I felt like I was in real danger of proving him right. I knew that if I were ever going to amount to anything, and if I were ever going to build a life for myself and Deloris, I would have to get out of my hometown. Although I was driven to never be like my dad, there was one way that I followed him—I enlisted in the Navy. Being only seventeen at the time, I had to get my parents' permission and have them sign for me. I told them my situation, and thankfully they understood. I hated to leave my mother, my sisters, and Deloris, but it was time for me to spread my wings and go out on my own.

It was December 1959. When it came time to go, I was excited. I was about to leave all my troubles behind and set off on an adventure while the rest of my friends would be living the same old humdrum, small-town life. At the same time, I was scared. I had never been away from home, never really been too far from my mother. But I was determined to do something with my life, and this was my shot.

I had no idea what I was getting into.

Chapter 2

My first stop in the Navy would be basic training in Chicago, Illinois. I took my first-ever plane ride to get there, all on Uncle Sam's dime. I was a bundle of nerves all the way there, and I am sure all the other guys were, too, but we did a decent job of not letting it show. They were all like me, looking for a way out, trying to find a path that would lead them to some success and adventure, and get them away from where they were from.

Once I got there and basic training started, I did not have time to be nervous. My drill instructors made sure none of us had much time to think about anything at all. Basic training was not all that hard for me, but what took some getting used to was the cold. I had lived through some rough winters down South, but the cold in Chicago was a completely different kind of cold. It seeped into my bones, and for the first several days, I shivered no matter how many layers of clothing I wore. Looking back on it now, Chicago was just a taste of the cold I would have to endure a few years later, but at the time, it was just about all I could stand.

About the time I got used to the cold in Chicago, I received orders to go to Naples, Italy. At least I would not have to bundle up there. I had only been outside of Georgia a few times, and

I had never been out of the United States. Now, within a few short months, I had flown in my first airplane, met folks from all over the country, and traveled far beyond any trip I had ever taken. Things were looking up, and I was excited to see what things were like in Italy. As excited as I was, nothing could have prepared me for that plane ride. I was still getting used to traveling by air at the time and was still just a little nervous. It was a twin-engine Navy cargo plane, a huge thing that I am sure they had used during WWII. Well, while we were flying out over the ocean, the plane developed problems with one of the engines. That is what they say when that kind of thing happens: "We've developed problems with one of the engines," because that sounds nicer than, "One of our engines just caught fire, and we could all die in a few minutes." The plane dropped so low I felt like I could stick my hand out the side and skim the surface of the ocean, but the pilot and co-pilot kept everything going, and we limped along on the remaining engine until we reached a place called the Azores. If you do not know where that is, do not feel bad. I did not either until I went there. It is a tiny island way off the coast of Portugal, about a ten-and-a-half-hour flight from Naples, Italy.

After all that, I was glad to see some dry land, and the Azores was it. We spent three days there while the engine was being repaired, but I did not have anything to do. Thankfully, I found a spot with some slot machines, so I played them to pass the time. I never did win anything, but it turned out to be a lot of fun. Going back up into the sky after almost crashing a few days earlier was scary, but I calmed myself down and boarded the plane. I was already about seventeen hours away from home back in Waycross, and I was about to go another ten and a half hours away to reach my new destination.

***

Chicago had been a big change for this country boy, but I didn't have time to venture off base during basic training. Italy, however, was a culture shock. The weather, the people, the old buildings—you could tell that place had a history that stretched way back before anything I had ever seen. It looked just like the pictures you would see in magazines or what you would see in movies and television shows, but this was altogether different. You could smell the exhaust from the cars, the sweat of people gathered in the outdoor markets in the middle of the day, and old men smoking their pipes out in front of little cafés. I have always been a car guy, and I will never forget those little cars in Naples when I first saw them. They looked like they would not hold a bag of flour from my family's general store, but somehow whole families of Italians crammed themselves in those little things and zipped all over town. They were good drivers, but they were also crazy drivers, at least compared to what I was used to. I could not believe how close some of them came to hitting each other, but they always got where they were going without a scratch. I had hoped to go on an adventure in the Navy and to see and experience things I could only have dreamt about back home, and I was finally here. Once or twice, I thought, *If only my friends and family could see me now!* Most of all, I felt like I was finally doing something with my life on my own terms. My dad's words of, "You'll never amount to anything," had faded a good bit, mostly because I was too busy doing instead of thinking. I missed my family, and I missed Deloris, but finally getting to Naples was a good feeling. I felt like I was not waiting around for life to happen to me.

As much as I wanted to explore the city, taste all the Italian food, and meet the locals, there was so much to do once I got settled and received my assignment. I was going to be in the communications department. It was not too bad of a job and mostly simple. When ships would enter the bay, I was part of a team that made sure they got all the supplies they needed; then, they would head back out to sea again. This was in 1960. They housed us in three-story tall barracks, and most of us just went to work on our assignments, stayed in the barracks, or explored the city. Those barracks had everything you needed, including a movie theater on the third floor.

Things hummed along normally most of the time until, one day, we were all watching a movie in the barracks. I cannot for the life of me remember what the movie was. All I remember was it was about halfway over, and I kept feeling my chair shake like somebody in the row behind me had put his foot on the back of my chair. We were all young men, so that would happen sometimes. Occasionally someone would annoy you just because they could, or one of your friends would distract you right when the best part of the movie was about to happen. Now, if you know much about Italy and geography and all of that, you might have already put two and two together. But I was thousands of miles away from home, and I never cared that much about my geography classes, so I just figured it was one of the guys behind me horsing around. Finally, I turned around and said, "Hey, friend, quit kicking my chair. I'm trying to watch the movie." I squinted a little so I could see his face, and he looked confused.

"What?" he said. "I wasn't kicking your chair!"

I had turned back around to watch the movie when I felt it again. I looked over my shoulder, and I could see that the guy behind me was looking around, too. We all were. Pretty soon, the floor started shaking underneath us. Somebody switched on the lights, and just as they did, we saw little cracks spread across the walls like fingers, only the cracks kept getting bigger.

To make it back to the first floor, you had to head down these big concrete flights of stairs. It did not take us long to find the door or to get down those stairs.

All of us got away from the building as quickly as we could, and we were astounded at what we saw. It was nighttime, and the barracks sat on a hill overlooking the Bay of Naples. We watched as transformers exploded on their poles one by one, showering everything with sparks all the way across town and out of sight, although we could hear them popping in the night. Small fires sprang up, and we watched as the red and orange flames licked up at the night sky while the smoke from the fires billowed up into the clouds. The ground kept shaking all this time; then, it was over as soon as it had started. Even so, we kept watching as the locals clogged the streets, trying to get out of town in case another one hit. I had wanted to get out of my hometown and have some life experiences but living through an earthquake was not anywhere on my list. I found out later that Naples has had some serious earthquakes over the years, but that was a minor one. The damage from that earthquake was not too bad, but it scared us nearly to death. It is a wonder nobody got trampled or knocked down the stairs on our way to the first floor. The Lord took care of the rest of those boys and me that night for sure, and I thank Him for that.

***

Not long after surviving the first and only earthquake of my life, I put in for leave to go home for a little while. Deloris and I had stayed in touch, even though it was hard to carry on a private conversation on the telephone at the barracks. Being on the other side of the world has a way of making you miss somebody, and we had decided to get married even if I could only come home long enough for the wedding. We were still young, but both of us knew we'd found the right one. Even so, we did not go into it without putting some serious thought into it. We both agreed that if we got married, divorce was not an option. It was us against the world. No matter what might happen between us or what hardships life might throw our way, we resolved to stay together through thick and thin.

When I got back home to the States, it was strange. I felt like I had seen so much that I was a changed man, and I was. It was good to come home and see all those familiar landmarks and see the people around town going about their lives just the same as they had when I had left. Even so, I was glad I had left. If I had not gone into the Navy, I do not know that I could have come back to Waycross and really appreciated it the way I did. It was like seeing it all for the first time. As nice as it was to be home, I had more important business to attend to than reminiscing about my hometown—namely, going to meet my soon-to-be bride at the church.

We were married on December 31, 1961, and we have been together ever since, just like we talked about. We had the same outlook on marriage, and I think that has seen us through a lot of troubled times, but without the help of God the Father, we would have never made it this far. Back then, I had not yet been called to His service, but He still reached down and brought Deloris into my life, and I thank Him for that. His love really is unconditional.

Since I had not been in the Navy for only a brief time, we didn't have much money to speak of, so we did the best we could with what we did have and spent a few days at the Waycross Motel, then we borrowed Deloris' dad's truck and headed to a nearby town where the fishing was good. Some women do not like to fish, but Deloris and I have always shared a common love of fishing and being around the water, so we stayed on the Little Satilla River and had a grand time, talking and fishing and just enjoying being with one another. That night we threw some blankets in the back of the truck and slept out under the stars. Some people spend lots of money on their weddings, then head off out of the country to exotic places for the honeymoon. That is fine, and I don't look down on folks who do that. But for Deloris and me, all that mattered was that we were together. It might not have been an extravagant wedding or honeymoon, but I would not trade it for the world. Everything was simply perfect.

***

Being a married man was a good feeling, but I did not get to stay with Deloris for long. Before I knew it, I was back in Italy. I finished my tour of duty without any more earthquakes or engine failures, but as soon as my tour was up, I was assigned to the USS Witek DDE 848 Destroyer escort out of Boston, Massachusetts. In Naples, I had seen plenty of Navy ships but had not gotten many chances to go aboard them, much less go out on the ocean in them. Going out on that ship for the first time was quite an experience. Our ship was much smaller than the destroyer, and it was our job to protect the destroyer and the aircraft carrier. That destroyer was first used in the late 1940s during WWII, named after a Marine who was posthumously awarded the Medal of Honor. Just like the old cargo plane that scared me to death when one of the engines went out on the way to Naples, it seemed like the ghosts of WWII were not that far behind me. It would be interesting to see if my dad had been on or around any of that same equipment when he was in the war, but I imagine those records are lost or stuffed in a cabinet somewhere.

Since this was the first time I had ever been out on the ocean in one of those Navy ships, I learned right away that those big boats handle the waves with ease. A destroyer is built to handle just about anything out there on the ocean and handle it well, but we were in the smaller ship that served as the escort. In case you do not know about Navy ships, I was on the smallest ship out of the whole bunch, and our ship did not handle the waves nearly as well as the huge destroyer or the aircraft carrier. For three months, I was so seasick I could barely perform any of my duties. Those three months are still one big blur to me, but I can remember sitting on the bathroom floor, hugging the toilet while one of my shipmates dropped a whole porkchop in the toilet bowl. The sight and smell of that food just made it worse, but I am glad he got a good laugh out of it. Guys can be tough on each other, but it is all in playful fun, and I don't hold it against him. Honestly, it would have been funny at the time if it had not been happening to me. After those three long months, I finally found my sea legs.

I missed my mother terribly, as well as Deloris, but during that time, I was only worried about what was in front of me because that was all that mattered. Things were getting serious for all of us in the service, especially the Navy, but we had no idea just how serious.

We conducted various battle station maneuvers, and they trained us well. Everybody had a job to do, and every job counted. Being part of the communications department in Naples had been a breeze compared to this, especially once I found out what my assignment was going to be: forward gun mount. When I first heard that, it sounded exciting. I would get to handle one of those big guns like in the movies. Now, if you have never been in the service and all you know about it is from watching movies, let me explain something about that assignment to you as it was explained to me. The officer in charge told me that my assignment meant I would be in the direct face of the enemy if we ever had to engage an enemy craft. This also meant I was never to leave my battle station unless I was ordered to do so by my commanding officer. My job was to stay put and stay on that gun, no matter how many torpedoes an enemy submarine fired or how many bombs an enemy aircraft dropped. The sole purpose in this world for all of us aboard that escort would be to protect the mother ship, the aircraft carrier, and to intercept the enemy if possible. These were not just training exercises—we were given these orders as though we were about to go into battle at any time. Up to this point, the Navy had been an enjoyable experience. The discipline and routine were good for me, and I learned a lot about giving and receiving respect, as well as how a supply chain works, how the chain of command works, and how it is just as important to be a good leader as it is to be a good follower. I am glad I was in the service, and it went a long way toward making me the man I am today. In some ways, it even taught me some valuable lessons about business. I was not afraid of fighting, but something about those orders gave me a bad feeling. I felt like I was on the wrong ship. Now that I was a married man, things were different. It was not all about me anymore, and I worried about what would happen to Deloris if I never made it home.

The reason that everything got serious so quickly was that it was around the time the Cuban Missile Crisis started really heating up in 1962. They just barely mention that in history classes today in schools, but at the time, everybody was worried. The Cold War was in full swing, and while Kennedy, Khrushchev, and Castro were fussing and fighting about nuclear missiles, many Americans were terrified that the Russians would put their missiles in Cuba—all pointed right at the United States mainland. Of course, it never happened, but that part of history had not been written yet, and it was anybody's guess as to how it would all pan out. Well, they did bring in some missiles, but Kennedy ordered a "quarantine" of Cuba so the Communists could not bring in any more ordnance or supplies. This kicked off the Cuban Blockade, and I was smack dab in the middle of it. The closest the world would ever come to nuclear war, and I was charged with fighting against the people who had already brought nuclear missiles into Cuba and wanted to bring in even more of them.

Being in the middle of all that had a way of putting things in perspective for me. Even so, I had enlisted, and it was my job to do as I was told and serve my country to the best of my ability, so I did my job without complaining. As uncomfortable as I was, I did not let it affect my performance, and I did my best not to let it show. I was not the only one who was worried because a lot of those boys on that boat talked about it.

Once the blockade was officially over in 1963, I was honorably discharged. I left with honor, as countless other former enlisted people have. God was working in my life, and I did not even know it. He put me on this path, and I have followed it. He knew what was in store for me, and I am grateful to Him for allowing me to experience my time in the Navy and for allowing me to come home when the time was right. His timing is always perfect. He knew it was more important for me to go home to my wife, and He set it all in motion.

I was glad to finally be going home, but I had no way of knowing that the home I would be going back to was different from the home I had left. I also had no way of knowing that one of the worst tragedies of my life was just around the corner.

Chapter 3

I was honorably discharged from the Navy in May of 1963 and made it back to Waycross, Georgia, as soon as I could. During my time in the Navy, I missed my home, but I especially missed my mother. As I have said, she was my best friend in the world, and I think that trying to save each other from my dad only strengthened that bond.

Once I was back home and settled, I re-adjusted to civilian life and took on odd jobs like bagging groceries and whatnot—whatever I could do to make some money for myself and Deloris. Even so, I made it a point to visit my mother every Saturday. These Saturdays were a blessing for me, and they were for her, as well. Deloris would usually come with me, and she and my mother got along so well. She really welcomed Deloris into the family and treated her like one of her own. I had been gone for so long, and mom and I had a lot of catching up to do. We would sit and talk for hours, and it became our special day. I looked forward to it every week, and it began a new tradition in our family.

Of course, not everything was as it should have been since my dad was usually there, drinking his half-pint of whiskey. He would join in the conversation here and there, then leave us alone without any problems. He was never out of the way with Deloris, thankfully, and did not let her see that side of him, although I had told Deloris some of what I'd had to endure growing up in that house. Even if I had not told her, she could feel the tension in the air anytime Dad was around.

Things kept on like this for a while, and everybody seemed to settle into this routine. Then Deloris and I decided to have supper at my parents' house on a Friday night instead of the usual Saturday. I do not remember why we moved the day, but as soon as we walked in the door, I knew something was wrong. It was not obvious at first. Everything looked the same, and my parents acted the same. It was just a gut feeling, and I tried to tell myself I was only tired from work or from worrying about bills, but the longer we stayed, the more I noticed a change in my dad. He had never been a very sociable man, but that night he seemed more standoffish than usual. He kept going to his bedroom for lengthy periods like he wanted to be alone. He kept this up for a little while, then came back into the living room, roaring about how my mother was sneaking around and seeing the breadman that delivered bread to the general store every week. It was the same old paranoia and baseless, drunken accusations as always. It broke my heart to see it again. For so long, my dad had at least kept himself from unleashing his rage in front of me, and now he was doing the same as he had always done, except this time, it was in front of my new bride. I felt embarrassed and ashamed, but Deloris understood. She knew I could not help who my dad was, and she knew I was nothing like him—I had made sure of that. Still, something was different about him that night, like he was building himself up toward something that he could not quite make himself do. Looking back at it now, I should have seen the signs, but at the time, no one could have known what he would do. I do not even know if he had any clue as to the evil he would soon inflict on us all.

***

Our little tradition of visiting with my mother continued for all of 1963. I was twenty-one years old and still trying to find my place in civilian life. Being back home was good, but it was also challenging. Good jobs were scarce, and I missed being part of something bigger than myself. The routine, the chain of command, and the camaraderie of the Navy had done me a world of good, and civilian life left something to be desired. I jumped on any opportunity I could to make some money and hung in there with some jobs I really hated, but it was worth it all to be able to provide for my wife. I was glad to be with her again, but now I was under a different kind of stress than I had ever known.

It was because of this that Deloris and I decided to stay home that Christmas Day in 1963. Normally, there would not have been much of a decision. We would have gone to my parents' house to spend the holidays with them, my sisters, and my grandmother. But for some reason, that year, we did not.

You never think about how a small, simple decision like that can change your life forever. What I am about to tell you is difficult for me to tell and even harder to relive, but I feel like I owe it to you to tell you the whole story and the true story—the good and the bad of my life. Believe me when I tell you that what happened that day was the single worst event in my entire lifetime.

It was the day after Christmas. Deloris and I were at our home, enjoying time with one another. The phone rang, and I picked it up, expecting to hear my mother on the other end of the line, asking how we were and inviting us to their house for supper later that day. She had been saved two weeks prior, and I was so happy for her. Knowing that we would one day walk together along the streets of gold in glory had brought us even closer together, and it had given us a lot to talk about.

Instead of being greeted by my mother, I heard one of my sisters on the other end of the line, out of breath, frantic. Her voice was shaky, as though she had been crying, and her speech tumbled out of her mouth all at once. It took me a moment to register what she was saying, but once it clicked in my mind, it felt like someone had punched me in the stomach. My dad had shot and killed my mother and grandmother right there in the house where I had grown up.

My sister was a wreck, but as she struggled to tell me more, I suddenly did not want to hear anything she had to say. I quickly told Deloris what had happened, and she immediately launched into prayer. But as my precious, supportive, and loving wife prayed for my family and me in the face of this tragedy, a numbness clawed its way through my mind and heart until I felt physically frozen in shock. It had taken all these years, but whatever evil my dad had carried within his heart from what had happened to him during the war—or he had carried it inside him all his life—finally unleashed itself. Somewhere deep in the back of my mind, I had known this day would come, but I had fought against that knowledge, hoping that maybe, just maybe, it wouldn't turn out that way. As soon as the shock had set in, a wave of red-hot anger washed over me. My mother—my sweet, caring, easy-going best friend in the whole world—had been taken from me, as well as my God-fearing, tough-as-nails grandmother. The world was a little dimmer now that these women were no longer in it, and my dad was the one to blame. He could have chosen to beat them, and that would have been bad enough. But to take their lives? What was even worse was that he had done it right in front of my sisters. It was unthinkable. It was unforgivable.

If I had time to think, that is all I would rather have thought, this is unforgivable, and that would have been the end of it. Instead, there was no thinking about it. The rage and anger burning within my soul compelled me to jump into action—I wanted to kill my dad.

As Deloris continued praying, I ran to our bedroom and stood in front of my nightstand. Without hesitation, I pulled open the drawer. There in the soft bedroom light gleamed my .38 caliber pistol, nestled between some pillowcases. We had trained with rifles and pistols in the Navy, and I had done my fair share of target practice here and there as a kid, but for the first time in my life, that gun took on an entirely new meaning. At that moment, everything seemed so simple: I would use that pistol to make my dad pay. I would make him pay for all the put-downs, all the beatings he had given my mother and me, all the uncertainty and doubt he had planted in my mind, all the love he never showed any of us, and now this ultimate betrayal—this ultimate evil—he had brought into our lives.

I remember the way the grip of the pistol felt in my hand as I wrapped my fingers around it. I remember the weight of it and how sure I was of what I was about to do with it. Since we never knew if children or relatives would come over to our place, I never kept that pistol loaded, so the bullets were lying loose on the nightstand under some pillowcases, hidden from view in case anybody decided to go poking around in there. With the pistol in one hand, I reached in with my other hand to find the bullets, but as soon as I did, Deloris was there. She put her hands on mine, keeping me from uncovering the bullets. This was a flat-bottomed drawer, but somehow the bullets rolled in the drawer, and Deloris covered them with the pillowcases. I maintain that this was an act of God because neither of us bumped the bullets or otherwise caused them to move like that. In a rage, I kept fighting, trying to get to the bullets, but Deloris would not stop. She saw the anguish and the anger in my eyes, and God was working through her to stop me from doing something that could never be undone. I realized what I was doing, and it felt like I had come up for air after being forced underwater for a long time. I threw the pistol back on the nightstand, but even as I tried to stop myself, all I could think about was finding my dad, so I could hurt him the way he had hurt me. I wanted to kill him. I wanted to rid the world of him finally.

A still, small voice came to me then, just like it is described in 1 Kings, chapter 19 of the Bible. The voice said, "No, you're not!" That voice could only have been the voice of God. All at once, my mind shifted from anger and revenge to deep sadness, tinged with the fearful reality of what I was about to do before I came to my senses. Killing my dad was not the answer. If anything, I would have been put away, and his crime would have carried over to me. Had God not intervened, I know that is exactly what would have happened that day. All blessings and praise to the holiest heavenly Father for sparing me from that.

With the help of God, I fought off the temptation of Satan because it was Satan who put that thought in my mind in the first place. To have added another sin onto the sins my dad had already committed would have made Satan cackle with delight, but God said, "No!" When God speaks, you better listen. He will never lead you astray, and He will never tell you something you do not need to hear. I had narrowly avoided a terrible decision, but there was no time to even feel relieved. We ran out to our old car and rushed to my parents' home, unsure of just what we would find when we got there.

***

We pulled up to my parents' house. I could see my dad through the windshield, being escorted through the front yard by two police officers. They had already placed him in handcuffs, and what struck me first was that he did not seem like my dad at all. He was never a big, scary, intimidating man—at least not physically—but he had always carried himself like he was the one in charge wherever he went. As the policemen led him to the patrol car in front of the house, however, he seemed like a lost, broken little boy. He kept his head down, refusing to look anybody in the eye. I do not know if he realized I was there yet, but he sure was not letting on if he did. Not once did he even turn toward me.

There were so many things I wanted to say to him then. Besides what I wanted to say, there were plenty of things I wanted to do. Again, if the Lord had not been with me that day, I know I would have attacked him and ended up in handcuffs along with him. Only by the grace of God did I keep my cool. By that time, the police officers had spotted me, and I heard one of them tell another one, "There's Tim. Stop him from going in."

I knew they wanted to keep me separated from my dad for fear of what I might do. Eventually, they let Deloris and me into the house. Today, there would be truly little chance of this happening, even in a small town. This sort of crime was not common in little old Waycross, Georgia, though, and is still rare today. Since the police all knew us and knew what had happened in that house, they must have made an exception for us. To this day, I appreciate that, although what I found inside will be seared into my memory as long as I live.

I found my dear mother lying on her back. I walked to her, still in disbelief, even as I saw the blood that had pooled around her. It was clear that she had been shot in the stomach. I did not know what else to do but sit there beside her. Before I knew it, I could barely see from all the tears in my eyes, and I sobbed like a little child. All the love I had for her, and all the love she had for me, and to see her like that—it was more than I could bear. Sitting there beside her, I prayed to God to help me get through this somehow. This was long before the Lord had spoken to me and called me into His service, but even then, I knew that the pain I was feeling could only be helped by the Great Physician. After a time, I wiped my eyes well enough that I could look around. It did not take long for me to spot my grandmother. She was lying on the floor, face down, not too far from my mother. She had been shot in the back. Later, the police who had worked the scene told me that my grandmother had been taking two of my younger sisters toward the back door, trying to escape, holding onto them by their wrists as she fled. According to the police, the shotgun my dad used had a tight enough choke so that it held a close pattern; otherwise, the blast would have hit my sisters as my grandmother tried to get them to safety. The police also told me that my mother and grandmother died instantly, and it was no use to add to my grief by thinking they had suffered. The Lord has a plan for all of us, and while I will never understand why He let my dad do what he did, I am grateful that neither of them suffered. If it had to happen, then it is best that it happened that way. I am especially grateful that my mother decided to give her life to Christ two weeks before she was killed. She was only forty years old. Her death is something I will carry for the rest of my days, but at least I know I will see her and my grandmother again in heaven. We will surely have a lot of catching up to do.

When it was all said and done, my dad confessed to both murders. He did not put up a fight, and there was no talk of "temporary insanity" or anything like that. At the age of forty-four, my dad simply accepted his life sentence as though it was the most natural thing in the world, and that was that.

In the wake of that tragedy, Deloris was my rock. She was there for me, as always. God knew what He was doing when He sent her to me because I do not know that I could have made it through that time without her. No one else could have comforted and supported me the way she did.

We arranged a double funeral for my mother and grandmother. It had to be done but getting everything in place was overwhelming. Grief wracked my body, heart, and mind. There was nowhere to go to get away from it. I have endured many setbacks and hardships since then, and I have had to watch loved ones be committed to the earth after the Lord called them home, but the pain I felt during that time was unique. It cut me deeper and lasted longer somehow since it was so sudden and so intense. I am sure that a lot of it had to do with the knowledge that my dad was responsible. To be honest with you, I harbored some dark, hateful feelings toward that man for a long time after that. It took a long time before I could stand to see his face again, but I did. But that happened much later. For now, I want to talk about happier things.

***

After I came back from the Navy, things were not so good when it came to my jobs. In fact, there were times when things looked pretty bleak. Before long, however, I fell into working with a company that had me doing electrical work for a couple of years, where I learned a great deal of the trade and got some experience under my belt before getting on with another outfit. I stayed on with the second company for two or three more years, but it was all non-union work. My friends and other men in the trade kept encouraging me to join the union. They made it sound like a good deal, so I began to take it seriously.

The only problem was you had to take a test to join the union. Now, I already had the experience, and I knew I was not a dummy. "Book smarts," as they say, were not really my thing, and I was somewhat nervous about taking the test to join the union, even though I had earned my GED while I was in the Navy. I did not have anything to lose, so I gave it a shot.

I made the two-hour drive from Waycross to Savannah, Georgia, to meet with the business agent. In case you are not familiar with that title, it is just a fancy way of saying he was the head representative of that local electrician's union. He was the big boss who decided when and where you would take the test. We got along well, and he set me up with my test. As excited as I was, I still worried about that test. Whenever it came up among my family and friends, I brushed it off like it was not anything special, but I still worried about it. I guess the years of my dad telling me that I would never amount to anything had left its mark on me, which was strange since I had already accomplished so much at such an early age. Thankfully, Deloris was supportive of my dreams. She has always been a reliable source of comfort whenever I've been feeling low or when I was up against what seemed like impossible odds, and this time was no different. She believed in me, and that helped me to believe in myself even more.

When the day finally arrived for me to take the test, I walked into the room and saw that it was full. I looked around the room and saw men of all ages, some of whom were much older than I was. Some of them had much more experience, and for a moment, I felt like I was out of place. I sat down and introduced myself to a few of the guys and learned that some of them were taking the test for the second and even third time! *Oh, boy*, I thought. *This is going to be a lot tougher than I thought.* I did not have much time to think about it, however. The test administrator came around not long after that, gave us his little speech about how everything would go, and started passing out tests. I worked through mine, focusing on doing my best, and tried not to let anything else bother me. If I passed, great. If I failed, then I would just come back and try again.

Afterward, they informed all of us that we would get a call to tell us our results, and that was it. I left out of that building feeling good about the whole thing, but those were some of the longest days of my life. They had given us a time frame for when the call would come through with the test results, but each time the phone rang, I jumped up to answer it just to be sure.

Finally, I was home one evening, and the call came in. The voice on the other end told me what the call was about, and I held my breath. In the end, it turned out I was worried about nothing at all—I had done great on the test, and they wanted to set a date to accept me as a member of the union. But that was not all. They also invited me to meet face-to-face with two important men in the union. After hanging up the phone, I felt relieved. Deloris was waiting to hear the news, and I was so proud to break it to her. We were moving up in the world!

Once I was accepted into the union, they sent me to Jacksonville, Florida, for a little while, then back up to a town in Georgia in the year 1969. That town was just a dot on the map, being smaller than even Waycross. At the time, though, they were building a huge nuclear plant just outside of that town, and there was plenty of work to do to get it up and going. The work site was about forty-five minutes or so from Waycross, so I was thankful to be working so close to home. After struggling for so long, it looked like things were finally falling into place. At least, that is what I thought at the time.

***

Being a union man was everything I had hoped it would be. Not only did I make more money, but the union made sure my pay rate was protected, my job was much more secure, and the working conditions were safer than some of the non-union jobs I'd had previously.

Working at the nuclear plant site was the first time I had ever brought in what I considered to be good money, and Deloris took notice of it, too. You may be thinking that she went out and got herself some fancy clothes or wanted to buy a new car, but that is not at all what was on her mind. She has never been the kind to spend money needlessly, and we share that trait. No, she had a serious reason for spending this money. She consistently set aside ten percent of our weekly household income for the sole purpose of tithing to the church. I had grown up in church, so I understood about tithing. I knew it was a good thing to give back to God, but when it came right down to it, I did not think it was the right move for us. Looking back on it now, I realize how wrong I was. God had done so much for us already. For starters, He had kept me safe while I was in the Navy. Even before that, He saw fit to put me together with the most wonderful wife a man could ever ask for. He had stopped me from killing my own dad in a fit of rage, and then He had comforted my mind and heart after the deaths of my mother and grandmother. Now He'd helped me to get on with the union and work not even an hour away from home. But, as I told you at the beginning of this story, I was not always the man

I am today. From my point of view, we finally had a financial foothold and any money going out the door had better be spent on necessities.

Deloris, on the other hand, saw the importance of tithing from the beginning. To her, this was a necessity, just like buying groceries, putting gas in the car, or paying the electric bill. She understood that while paying the bills kept us clothed and fed, the tithes were for our spiritual health. This was the first real disagreement we had ever had. We had agreed that she would oversee the finances for our little family, so she was in charge of paying the bills and such, but I remember telling her to stop paying tithes to the church. She did as I asked, but she did not let it go without letting me know how she felt about it. "We can't afford to stop paying our tithes," she said. "But because you are the head of the house, I'll listen to you and stop paying tithes on your income. But I want you to know it is wrong to stop paying tithes because God has always blessed our faithfulness in His ability to take care of us."

True to her word, she stopped taking out tithes from the money I was making, but we had not agreed to anything that affected her income. Quietly, without any fuss and without making a scene about it, she continued to work and send ten percent of her own income to the church as a tithe. Within a year, we welcomed the birth of our second son, and over the course of the next four years, my income from the nuclear plant job increased substantially. By that time, I realized I had been wrong about tithing. What I saw as an expense was really a way of giving back to God, who, in turn, gave back to us. Like I said at the start of this book, nothing I have in this world is truly mine. God has given me everything I have, and it is only right to give back to Him because it all came from Him in the first place. Deloris was right all along, and I finally came around to her way of thinking. After that, I started tithing and even back-paid the tithes I had missed. I saw a noticeable increase in the blessings God bestowed upon my family and me, even beyond what He had already done for us. It turns out you cannot outgive God because He's already given you life and the path to eternal salvation. He blessed me before that, and He has never let up since then. I did not know it then, but He was about to bless me soon after that by saving me from certain death.

***

Remember much earlier in my story, when I told you about my grandmother on my dad's side and what she told me when I was seven years old? Well, along this time, I received a call that she was in the hospital. She was elderly by then, and I had heard that she did not have much longer to live. I wanted to see her one last time, but I could not get off work immediately. I finished my day's work, jumped in my truck, stopped by my home, and rushed to the hospital with Deloris by my side.

I walked into my grandmother's room. The EKG machine monitoring her heartbeat kept a steady, soft beat in the background. Over my lifetime, I have seen death come to many people. There is a feeling you get when you are in the presence of someone who knows the end is near. Sometimes you can feel that person's fear, regret, or pain when they realize they did not live their lives the way they should have. That, however, was not the case with my grandmother. No, she was at peace. She had lived the life of a virtuous, God-fearing woman, and she was ready to meet her heavenly Father.

My sisters and other family members had already visited her, but she had been waiting for me, specifically. I thought back to what she had told me when I was just a little child, and it all clicked in my head. It was a Wednesday, and almost the exact time of day she had mentioned all those years ago. I knew that sometimes people would hold onto life just long enough to see one special person, and I also knew that she was ready to go to her heavenly home in glory. For that reason, I told her, "I release you, Grandmother." It was my way of letting her know I was there and that she could "take her flight" when she was ready, just as she had predicted in 1949. With those words, she seemed to drift off into a gentle, peaceful sleep. The EKG machine buzzed. Deloris and I looked to see that the readout on the machine had flatlined. As saddened as I was to see my grandmother go, I knew she was now safe in the arms of the Father. I glanced over at the clock. It read exactly seven o'clock. What a blessing it is to know the exact time you will depart this world. Just as she described, I received the "double portion," just like Elijah did with Elisha. Today, I often think about the other half of what she told me when I was a child. She did not get to see Christ's triumphant return, but she believed that I would. She was right about the time she would depart this old world, and she was right about my double portion. Who is to say she was not right about me getting to see Christ return? If it is the will of the Father, then I certainly welcome that wonderful sight.

***

During my first few years of working for the union, I befriended a person from Waycross by the name of Jack. He was married with two kids, and they would all come over to our place sometimes, and other times we would go to their home. We grew close to them, and they were great people.

Jack and I shared a love of fishing, and we often went on fishing trips together, usually just in my little jon boat. I was twenty-six years old, and while I still did not have much in the way of material possessions, I still felt like I was rich. With my own boat, a good fishing friend, and time off to go fishing, I felt like the luckiest man in the world. We never got into deep-sea fishing with those big, fancy boats and equipment, but it did not matter because what we had was plenty good enough for us. Back in those days, regulations were not as strict as they are now, so we never wore life jackets and safety gear, although I imagine we had some stowed away just in case. We would usually just go fishing in our regular clothes.

Jack and I planned a fishing trip for White Oak Creek near Kingsland, Georgia. It is about an hour south of Waycross, not too far from Daytona Beach, Florida. Right after planning the trip, I started smelling this awful smell. It smelled like something was burning, but not the way a fire smells. It was a rancid, nasty, burning smell that came and went, and I started searching all through our house, trying to find where it was coming from. I asked Deloris if she smelled it too, and she just looked confused. Every time I asked her about it, she said she did not smell anything. She thought I was teasing her or trying to play a joke on her because she eventually told me, "No, I don't smell anything. You just need to go and blow your nose." At first, I thought it was something in the house, but then I started smelling it in my truck and at work. I thought something was wrong with my nose, and I even considered going to the doctor to get checked out.

As the date of the fishing trip approached, a strange feeling came over me. Remember how I said I never took any special gear on a fishing trip other than just what we needed to fish? Well, for some reason or another, I felt driven to get a pair of rubber boots for the trip. It was the strangest thing, but it did not stop there. I got the boots, but I also picked up a life jacket, then set to work on the boat itself. First, I cut some two-by-fours and used them to insulate the aluminum boat from the motor. At the time, I figured it was just the electrician part of my mind needing a project to work on. Once that was done, I insulated the sides of the boat, all the way down, where you might put your hand to grab the side of the boat when you are out on the water. I did not know why I was doing this, but I worked on it with diligence and seriousness. That horrible smell would not leave me alone, but I shrugged it off and chose to focus on relaxing on the water and spending some time with Jack.

When the time came for the trip, we loaded up and headed for White Oak Creek. It was not too hot or too cold, and there was not a cloud in the sky. I remember thinking it was the perfect day for fishing. Jack and I were in good spirits, and everything seemed right with the world. If he mentioned anything about my recent additions to the boat, I do not recall him saying anything. The only thing on our minds was getting the boat in the water and filling it up with as many fish as we could catch.

We arrived right on time, put in, and got down to it. I had packed my life jacket and rubber boots several days before, and I figured that if I had brought them, I might as well wear them. We hit several spots throughout the day but never caught anything. Naturally, we were bummed out about our lack of success, but one of the things I have always enjoyed about fishing is just being out there. I know people who like to go deer hunting, and they say something similar. It is not always about bagging the biggest buck. Sometimes it is just enough to be out there in nature, away from the towns and cities, and everything moving so fast with so much to do and so little time. Everything moves slower out there, and life is simpler and more meaningful. We were enjoying that part of it for sure, but we still wanted to catch something, so we agreed to head to one more location before we called it quits. On the way to the final fishing spot, I noticed one small cloud scudding across the sky, but neither of us paid it any mind. It did not look big enough to carry much rain, anyway. Still, it followed us as we arrived at our final fishing spot for the day. Before long, we passed directly under that cloud. What I am about to tell you might be hard to believe, but I promise you it happened.

Just as the boat passed directly under that little cloud, a bolt of lightning snaked down from it and caught Jack on the shoulder. It all happened before I realized what was going on, and I did not have time to grab him, warn him, or do much of anything. The impact from the lighting threw him backward toward me, and as he fell, he hit his head on a five-gallon bucket we kept in the boat for any fish we might catch. Now, if you are not an electrician, you may not understand what happened to me. About the same time that the lighting struck my friend, I found myself down in the boat, curled up into the fetal position. Electricity has been known to "draw" a person, meaning it can make you pull your arms and legs up toward your body as if its energy is making you compress yourself to get away from it. This is exactly what happened to me. Jack ended up on his back at the bottom of the boat, and there I was, curled up, wearing my rubber boots and life jacket. As soon as it happened, it was all over. The cloud hung above us, looking strange and out of place in an otherwise cloudless sky. I looked down at Jack, horrified. His skin was burnt black from the lightning strike, unrecognizable. His hair had been singed, and his shirt had torn where the lightning had struck him, but what scared me the most was the smell. I realized I had smelled it before, and then it hit me—the horrible odor I had smelled for the past two weeks was the smell of burnt flesh. I have never smelled it since that day.

For a moment, I just sat there, unsure of what to do and unsure if it was all a dream. Surely, I did not just watch my friend die. I stood and felt the boat rock a little with my movement. A slight wind caught my face, and I knew this was all too real. Everything was completely silent. Then I turned, started the motor, and headed back to the shore.

Once I got back, I found someone close to the shore. I must have looked a little silly with my life jacket and rubber boots since few people wore all that garb just to go fishing around those parts. But when he saw my face, he knew I was serious.

I told him what had happened, and together we loaded my friend in my truck. I thanked the man who helped me with Jack and asked him if he had any idea of what to do. I was still in shock from what happened, and it is not every day your friend gets killed by lightning, so I was at a loss as to how to handle the situation. He was not too sure, either, but he gave me directions to the sheriff's department, where I could take the body and tell my story. I thanked him and drove to the sheriff's department, completely dumbfounded.

All my life, I have always respected the law. The deputies I spoke with that day, however, did not make a good impression on me. There I was, still reeling from the loss of my friend, thankful to God that I was spared from such a freak accident, looking for help from the local authorities, and all they wanted to do was interrogate me. They must have kept me there for four hours, questioning me on everything under the sun.

They wanted to know how I knew Jack, if I had any firearms, if there had been any conflicts between us, if we had been using drugs, or if we had been drinking—on and on and on. Eventually, I told them about the fellow that helped me on the shore and said he could serve as a witness if necessary. They kept implying that I had somehow killed Jack. They figured that I somehow knew when and where the lightning would strike and used my electrical knowledge to protect myself from it. I wound up having to get a lawyer involved, but once the coroner made his examinations, they all lost interest in me as a suspect. I imagine all of them have retired by now, but they sure did not oversee that situation well, at least from where I was standing. In their defense, though, that was the first time they had ever seen anything like that. I was from out of town, so maybe they jumped to the first conclusion that came to mind. When you think about it, though, the truth was stranger than any scenario they could think up.

Not long after it happened, I took some time to reflect on the death of my friend. I recalled that when I was talking with the deputies, I no longer smelled the horrible smell of burning flesh that had hounded me for the two weeks before the fishing trip took place. I looked back on those odd ideas to get the rubber boots and the life jackets and to insulate the boat. These things were completely out of character for me. I had never thought about doing any of that until that trip, and I have not done anything like that since. It occurred to me that God, because of His infinite wisdom, which allows Him to see and know all things, saw fit to warn me about what would happen. Not only that, but He put the idea in my mind to insulate the boat and to wear rubber boots to protect myself. I was told later that, had I not insulated the motor from the aluminum boat, the lighting could have caused the motor to explode and kill me.

In a way, the deputies were right. I had taken the necessary steps to protect myself from a lightning strike. The only problem was there was no way to know exactly when and where lightning would strike. I guess a meteorologist could tell you where it is likely to happen, but no one knows exactly where and when it will strike. Well, there is one who knows, and that's God the Father. For some reason, He planted that instinct in my mind and made sure I survived that ordeal. Satan once again had come to claim my life, but God said, "No!" just as He had that day when He stopped me from taking revenge on my dad.

As He tells us in Romans 12:19 (KJV): "Vengeance is mine." He spared me then just like He spared me from the lightning, and through that event, He had shown me His power. More than that, He showed me that He had selected me for things greater than my own human ambitions and desires. No one knows the full extent of His plan, and I am not one to question Him. As a younger man, I did from time to time, but now I simply do His will as best as I can. At the time, however, I tried to find some meaning in what happened. It was obvious to me that He was trying to show me something, but I did not understand Jack's place in all of it. Jack was a good man as far as I knew him, and I knew him well. His wife was a good person, too. If Jack had been an awful human being, I could understand why it was his time to depart from this life. As much as I might wrestle with those questions, at the end of the day, it is all beyond my understanding. I still wish things had turned out differently and that the message God was trying to send me could have been communicated in some other way. Life is like that sometimes, though. Good people die, and bad people prosper—or seem to prosper. It was the same with my mother and grandmother. Neither of them had done anything to deserve what happened to them. There was not a strand of evilness in their hearts. Still, their lives were cut short, and I was left to grieve for them just as I grieved for my friend. The Lord knew what He was doing, and I passionately believe He has a purpose for everything that happens in this life. It was just Jack's time. Once again, God had said, "No," and spared my life.

After it was all said and done, I was the one to deliver the news to Jack's wife and two children. It was hard standing on that front porch, looking that woman in the eye, and telling her that she'd never see her husband again in this life. I felt sympathy for her since my own mother and grandmother were taken from me so suddenly. The death of a loved one is always difficult, but somehow, it is even harder to bear when you do not have a chance to say goodbye. Jack's wife later went on to marry a preacher, and the last I heard of them, they were doing well. I will never forget my friend, and I hope to see him again one day. I still miss our talks and the time we spent together.

Even so, God spared me that day. Once again, He had said, "No!" when I could have easily been taken from this earth.

***

I continued working on the big plant job close to home through 1974. My work life and family life hummed right along until one day, toward the end of my time at that job, I received a phone call at work. It was Deloris, and her news was not good at all—our house was on fire.

When I came home and saw my home reduced to rubble, it made me physically sick. We had been married for twelve years at that time, and we had weathered some difficult storms together, but we had to lean on one another extra hard now that our home was destroyed. Everything we had worked so hard for had literally gone up in smoke. Things had been going so well for us, but now we would have to start all over.

Thankfully, Deloris' parents opened their home to us, but I have never been one to impose, even in such serious circumstances. Deloris contacted a friend who owned a vacant mobile home not too far away, and he agreed to let us stay there until we could get back on our feet and build a home. Again, just when things looked grim, the Lord stepped in and helped us through our time of trouble. It was not the perfect solution to our problem, but at least we had a place to stay, and we did not have to worry about imposing on family and loved ones, although Deloris' parents would have let us stay there for as long as we needed.

After the fire, I tried to find more work locally, but the work had dried up. We had put some money aside to live on, but we still needed to feed our two sons. The breaking point for me came soon afterward. Not everything had been destroyed in the fire. Out of what little was left, Deloris had salvaged some clothes, and she had set herself to the task of cleaning the smoke smell and soot out of them as best as she could. The clothes smelled awful. Someone had mentioned to her that bleach would be her best bet for getting the smell out of those clothes, but as hard as she tried, she just could not make it work. She worked so hard on it for so long, trying to keep us from spending our quickly dwindling money on new clothes, but all that bleach made her hands bleed.

At that point, I'd had enough. If there was no workaround where I lived, it was time to go wherever the work could be found, even if that meant leaving my family behind for a while. I needed money, and I needed to build a new house for my family. My back was against the wall. To say I was desperate was an understatement, but it is amazing what you can do when you have to reach down deep and dig yourself out of that kind of situation. People talk about being in your "comfort zone," but much of my life up until that point had been anything but comfort. I had finally established a kind of comfort zone, and now I was kicked out of it like a baby bird being pushed out of the nest. Again, God was there for me. He made a way for me, that is for sure. He never said the way would be easy, though.

With no other options close to home, I called around to everyone I knew to see if there were any jobs in the Southeastern United States. No success there, so I finally called up the business agent. He looked around for me, but he could not find anything either. I was disheartened. This was the man who knew where the jobs were, and he could not find one, at least not anything that would be worth going to for a man in my situation. Finally, he got back to me and said he had found something. I was overjoyed until he told me where I would have to go. My heart dropped when he said the name of the state: Alaska. All I knew about Alaska was it was freezing cold, there were bears out there that could about swallow you whole, and I remembered some pictures of igloos and some of the Native American people that had lived there since before Columbus ever arrived. Just as I got over the shock of potentially going to Alaska for work, the business agent hit me with another bombshell. He knew there was work out there, but he said he could not promise me that I would get on at any of those jobs.

For just a moment, it seemed like there was no way out. I thought about Deloris and my sons, stuck in that mobile home for the rest of our lives. Now, I was tremendously grateful to Deloris' friend for letting us stay there, but it was under the agreement that we would only be there temporarily. If I could not get work, we would eventually be out on the streets. My dad's words echoed in my mind: "You'll never amount to anything." That was Satan taunting and toying with me, disrupting my mind, and trying to stop me, and he was doing a fine job of it. I knew this was the only option available to me; it was do or die, even if there was no guarantee that anything would come of it.

I told the business agent that I would go for it and that I fully understood there was no promise of work. He said he would help me as much as he could, and I thanked him and hung up the phone. Uncertain about my future and the future of my family, I took enough money out of the bank to live on for a few days once I had reached my destination. Deloris and I prayed about it and trusted in God to pull us through, just as He had seen us through the financial, emotional, and physical storms we had endured so far.

Chapter 4

True to his word, the business agent set everything up for the long journey to Alaska. I would be flying out of Waycross in a little twin-engine plane for the first leg of the trip, and the sight of those two engines conjured up flashbacks to the engine trouble I had experienced in the Navy. Part of me wished I were back in the Azores, where it was warm and calm.

I climbed onto the plane and took my seat. I remember looking out the window to see Deloris outside, crying. Just beside her stood my sons, crying as well. The passengers had not finished being seated yet, and I guess the flight attendant saw what was going on because she asked if I wanted to get off the plane and see my family one last time before we took off. I appreciated her kindness, but I only told her, "No, thank you. If I get off this plane, I won't ever get back on." I turned my face away from her, trying to hide the tears that welled in my eyes. I am sure she had seen this many, many times before because she only nodded and let me be. Surrounded by all those people on the plane, I felt so alone. I could not even bring myself to look out the window at Deloris and the kids again. It just hurt too much to leave them. I was leaving them to try and get us on our feet again, but my heart hurt just the same.

Before long, the plane taxied down the runway, and we took to the sky. Once again, I found myself leaving behind everything I had ever known and everyone I had ever loved.

***

We stopped off in Atlanta, Georgia, where I switched over to a much bigger plane for the second leg of the trip, which ended in Washington State. The weather there reminded me of the first real cold I had experienced in Chicago, but I knew that Alaska would be a new kind of cold. Boy, was I right.

It seemed like it took us longer to get to Anchorage, Alaska, than it did to go from Georgia to Washington. I had made sure to bring just enough money for a cheap place to stay and a meal a day for several days. If that money ran out, I would be on the streets in a city that was 3,600 miles away from home, without any contacts and without any hope of getting back to Georgia. Remember that this was long before cell phones and way before the internet, so if I ran out of money, I could not even use a pay phone to call Deloris for help. Even if I did, what was she supposed to do? We had just enough left in the bank to feed her and the kids for about that long, anyway, so there was no going back if I was not successful.

My first stop was the union hall, but they did not have any work for me. I was disappointed, to say the least, but I was still hopeful. I asked around and found the cheapest hotel so I could be close to the union hall, then went and bought up some of the cheapest groceries I could get. There was no telling what would happen, and I had to prepare for the worst even as I was hoping for the best.

The next day, I got up, still worried but optimistic. I walked the frigid streets of Anchorage, bundled up so thick I could barely move. Even then, the cold crept in. Chicago was nothing compared to this. If you are from a cold place in the world, you might find this funny, but it was rough on this Georgia boy. Once again, I went into the union hall and asked if there was any work. Once again, I was told there was none.

This went on for three days. Anchorage was an interesting place, but as much as I wanted to explore the city, there was no money for that. My tiny motel room seemed a little smaller each time I entered it. I felt like I was going stir-crazy from just going to the union hall and back to the motel. Your mind has a way of playing tricks on you when you are as stressed and worried as I was, and you'd better believe I was beginning to get more than a little worried on the fourth day.

The walk to the union hall seemed to take a few more steps that day. When I walked in, they knew who I was and what I was there for, but there was an unusual look in their eyes when they saw me that day. At first, I thought it was just my mind playing tricks on me, but thanks to our heavenly Father, I was greeted with the news I had been waiting to hear since I had left Georgia. The dispatcher said he had a call for a job at Fort Wainwright in Fairbanks, Alaska. I told him I would be glad to take the job. It was all I could do to keep from jumping up and down with excitement right there in the union hall! From what I could tell, the pay would be just what I had been looking for. No matter how hard the work was or how dirty the working conditions were, I had found a way out. All my worry and doubt lifted as if the Lord had taken that burden off my shoulders.

I had trusted in Him to see me through, and He had. That is one of the lessons I have learned through the years—God is always there for you, even when you do not think He is. He will see you through even the darkest of times if you just lean on Him and trust in His mercy and wisdom. It amazes me how He has pulled me out of the fire repeatedly, and each time I look back and think of how silly I was to worry at all about whatever problem I had at the time. Then again, that is the way people are. Sometimes you cannot help but worry, and He knows that. That is why He is there.

Fairbanks was about an hour from Anchorage by plane. For a guy who had never set foot inside an airplane until he was seventeen years old, I was sure making up for the lost time. I found out that Fort Wainwright had been an Air Force base used during World War II. Its primary use at the time was as a cold weather test station since the Air Force did a lot of research out there to evaluate how below-freezing temperatures affected the planes and equipment, and they tested out all kinds of cold-weather clothing for the soldiers, as well. While I was there, I could see why they would have chosen that place to evaluate for sub-zero temperatures. It seemed like everywhere I had been since I left Atlanta just kept getting colder and colder. The connection Fort Wainwright had with the military and with World War II made me think about my dad again. It was like he was a ghost, following me around whether I wanted him to or not. Even in Alaska, with so many more important things on my mind, there he was. I stayed busy, though, and did not let it bother me. Just like in the Navy, they made sure I had plenty to occupy my time. I was only there for a few months before being transferred to what they called the "Old Man Camp." It was a funny name to call a place, but I did not laugh when they told me this latest transfer would put me just south of the Arctic Circle, near Kanuti National Wildlife Refuge in Interior Alaska.

There I was, thinking Fort Wainwright was about as cold as you could get. Turns out I still did not have a clue about the true meaning of the word "cold," at least not yet.

***

What they called the "Old Man Camp" turned out to be a support camp for the workers on the pipeline. They had told me it was close to the Arctic Circle, and when I got there, I believed it.

By now, I had wised up a little bit when it came to dressing for the Alaskan climate. Back home, I had a few jackets and one heavy coat that I'd only needed to wear for a month or two out of the whole year. Winters in South Georgia are usually mild and rainy, and it is rare to see any snow. In fact, everybody takes pictures of it and talks about it for years afterward when light snow comes around once every ten or fifteen years or so. That gives you an idea of what I was used to, but now that I had been in Alaska for a while, I had some of the heaviest, best-insulated coats I have ever had in my life, plus gloves, thermal undershirts and underpants, and earmuffs—the whole nine yards. It was a necessity up there for most of the year. Even so, I never really got used to it. I do not know that you ever do unless you were born and raised in that part of the world.

During my first winter in the Old Man Camp, it was not unusual to see the temperature drop to sixty-five degrees below zero with a wind chill factor of over a hundred degrees below zero. This was a wild, unforgiving place, and I became conscious of just how important it was to take care of yourself there. If you did not watch out, you would get frostbite or pneumonia, and it is safe to say you are done as far as work at that point.

Speaking of work, we sure had plenty of it at the Old Man Camp, especially since they were still building the place when I first arrived. I say "they" were building the place, but really it was all of us workers who were charged with doing a good bit of the construction. In a way, it reminded me of being in the Navy again. We had barracks and a mess hall, but there was no movie theater to be found, unfortunately. At least we did not have to worry about earthquakes in that part of the world. Since I was an electrician, I was on a crew that ran conduits from our barracks to the generator building. Think about that. This is a place so cold and so treacherous that you must build an enclosed, insulated building around it just to keep it warm enough to operate year-round! But in a place like that, it all made sense because, without that generator, we would not have lasted long. We were miles away from the nearest town of any size, and it was nighttime all the time. The barracks were not as cozy as the ones I'd had in Naples. I would crank up the heat in my room and cover up under layers of thick blankets until I was comfortable, but that ended as soon as I stepped out into the hallway. There was no heat in the long hallway, so chunks of ice hung on the walls day in and day out. That hallway led to the communal shower, so anytime you needed to wash off the grit, sweat, and grime of working, you'd have to warm yourself up in your room, run as fast as you could down the hall, shower as quickly as possible to keep the hot water from running out, then race back to your room. The bathroom was heated, but we all dreaded that freezing hallway.

Things were even less glamorous when it came to running the wire and conduit to the generator building. We had to set up a tent over the cables and keep the wire warm by way of electric "salamander" style heaters so it would stay flexible enough for us to work with it. Once we started working with it, we had to make sure we always wore our gloves because the frozen pipe was so cold that any exposed skin would immediately stick to it. It was the same way with door handles and other metal objects everywhere up there. To make things even more difficult, we could never stop pulling the wire once we got started, even for a few seconds. If we did, the insulation would freeze to the pipe, and the wire would crack if we tried to restart the pull. This meant we would have to start all over again, and more importantly, whoever slipped up and let it happen would be looking for another job by the end of the day. You'd better believe I was going to make sure I was not the one that let it happen, and all the guys on the crew felt the same. Once again, it reminded me of when I first joined the Navy, surrounded by guys from all levels of society that were trying to better themselves and some who were running away from something. When it came to working in Alaska, a lot of us were there because we could not find work closer to home, and this was the last resort. It was a do-or-die situation, and none of us wanted to waste that opportunity since most of us had families back home who were depending on us. Whenever I wanted to give up, or I would ask myself what I was doing in such a rough place, I only had to think of Deloris and the kids. That is who I was working for. If I had to endure the freezing cold and the tedious, physically demanding work, then so be it. I kept thinking that this would not last forever, that it was just a stepping stone to other, better things, and at the end of the day, it was all worth it for my family.

The job at the Old Man Camp lasted a full year. It was stressful, demanding work, but once it was over, they transferred me to the oil fields of Prudhoe Bay. I stayed there for six or eight months, and once that job was up, they transferred me again to Valdez, Alaska, where I worked on the oil storage tanks. There was an explosion of work in that area back in those days. Valdez was not a big city, and there were more men working in the camp than the entire population of the city.

The overall working conditions were not as bad in Valdez. For one, it did not seem to get as cold as it had been at Fort Wainwright or the Old Man camp. Then again, I was just getting used to it. Another thing I noticed was that it rained much more in Valdez than in other places I had been in Alaska. One good thing about working there was that I did not feel as isolated. In my downtime, I decided to explore the area a little. There were plenty of bodies of water around there, and you will not be surprised to hear that I bought a twelve-foot aluminum boat and a small motor to take advantage of that. While the work was hard in Alaska, I will say that it has some of the prettiest landscapes I have ever seen. I come from a place that is flat, so to see snow-capped Alaskan mountain peaks off in the distance was a real treat.

There was not much to see in the city of Valdez, but I remember there was a cab driver in town that I befriended. He was a talkative guy, and it was not long before he mentioned gold. I knew there had been a gold rush around those parts a long, long time ago, but I was surprised to hear that people were still finding gold around there. Little by little, he mentioned that he had found some, and once he was comfortable enough with me, he revealed that it was quite a bit. I did not know what to think. He was just making conversation, or he wanted me to think he was some big shot, but it did not make sense for a guy who had a chunk of gold in his possession to be driving a cab. It took some time, but he eventually showed the gold to me. He brought it in an old, two-pound metal coffee can, and when he pulled off the lid of the can, there sat the gold. That can was filled to the brim with little golden nuggets, and I asked him what he planned to do with it. "I want to sell it, of course," he replied. "But nobody I've talked to can afford what I'm asking." I tried to hide my shock when he told me the price, and I told him I would have to check around and see if it was a fair price since I did not know the first thing about the value of gold. It was the first time I had seen actual gold in real life. I asked around and found out that, sure enough, that was a fair price for that much gold. I just did not have that much money since I was sending home the majority of what I was making. I imagine that all the workers were doing the same thing, so nobody had that kind of cash. Looking back, I wish I had saved up and bought that gold from him. It would be worth much, much more than that today.

During my expeditions, I was amazed to find a little waterfall. This was during the winter, and the waterfall was mostly frozen over, but I staked out a claim there and registered it with the government offices based out of Anchorage. Since I could not afford the cab driver's gold, my plan was to try and find some gold myself, just like people had done up there a hundred years before. It encouraged me to know that people were still finding it here and there. The way I saw it, I was making money working the job there, and I could get in a little adventure and sightseeing, plus maybe find some gold and make even more money. Why not? It seemed like a great plan. I do not like sitting around without anything to do, so it was a terrific way to pass the time and gave me a project of sorts to work on.

I rigged up my own little dredge close to the mouth of the waterfall, thinking it would be a good place to look for any deposits of gold that came down the stream. Well, that plan seemed solid until the summer came along. I had never seen the waterfall in the summertime, and I should have put two and two together. Instead, I came back to my spot and was in for a rude awakening. I stood close to the waterfall, and my heart dropped. It had thawed out and turned into a miniature Niagara Falls. The coursing water had beaten my little dredge to a pulp, so much so that there was no way to repair it. I just shook my head and decided to go fishing instead.

**

Even though my gold prospecting days were now over, that did not mean I could not take advantage of the country. Alaska is gorgeous during the warmer months, and it was really something to be there in the middle of it all. After such a long, hard, dark winter, it was like the world had come to life suddenly. Streams ran with clear water that sparkled in the sunlight, whereas just a few months ago, that same water was locked up in ice, and the sun only peeked up into the sky for a few hours and went back down like it was scared. I saw all kinds of wildlife up there, but my least favorite would have to be the mosquitoes. Now, I was no stranger to mosquitoes. Being from South Georgia, you quickly get used to them. The summer months back home are muggy and blisteringly hot, and you will be washed down in sweat just from walking from your front door to your car in August. The mosquitoes will home in on you and will not give you any relief. But these Alaskan mosquitos were a whole different breed. Some of them were about as big as my hand, and I am not exaggerating too much about that. When they bit you, you sure knew you had been bitten.

My favorite animals up there were the bears. They had all kinds up around Valdez: black bears, brown bears, Kodiaks, and grizzlies. It is bear heaven up there, and I saw them at their scariest as well as at their friendliest.

My first encounter with those bears had been back during the winter. Since there were more men in the camp than there were people in the town, there was a good amount of food and supplies around. The bears would wander around just outside the camp from time to time, but they would rarely ever come inside the camp itself. The company hired a team of guys to try and control the bear problem, which is funny since you cannot really control a bear. These men had high-powered rifles loaded with some strong tranquilizer darts since it was against the law to outright kill them, even back in those days. It made sense to me. Animals are animals, and they are going to do what they do. If a bear comes sniffing around your camp for food, he is just doing what God made him to do, and there is no sense in killing him for it. Those animals were smart. Many of them would raise up on their hind legs and come down with their front paws to open the doors, just like a person. Now, that is a sight to see. It was rare for one of them to come into the camp, but when they did, those guys made sure to bring them down with their tranquilizer darts, then they would relocate the bear. The game warden and other officials got involved at that point, too. Well, it was all a good enough plan, except for one minor problem. Somehow, whoever mixed up the tranquilizer darts had either made them too strong, or they were made for bigger bears than the ones that wandered into the camp here and there. When it was all said and done, several of those bears ended up dying on the spot or later when they were being relocated. To be clear, those guys did not mean to kill any of those bears at all. It was their job to protect them by tranquilizing them and relocating them. It was just an unfortunate accident. We did not think much of it all winter, as we had a lot of work to do. When summer came around, however, we were in for a shocking surprise. Once the weather warmed up, we found ourselves swarmed by bears. At one point, they took over the camp. We had to evacuate everybody, and the game warden and federal people showed up. It was a mess. Now, I am no expert on bear behavior, but here is what I heard about it later. The bears that had been accidentally killed back during the winter must have been females, and the ones that swarmed us in the summer were their mates, who came down out of the hills and the forests looking for them. That is what drove them to the camp. All we knew was we were not about to share a bunk with a grown bear!

I remembered that event later when I took to fishing in small streams around Valdez. I had just caught my first salmon, and I was excited. Well, I came to my senses quickly when I noticed some of the largest bears I had ever seen, not that far away from me. They were fishing too, and it looked like they were doing a sight better than I was. After realizing just how big those animals were, I decided to let them have it. From then on, I made sure to keep my fishing activities out on the open ocean.

During my time in Alaska, I was allowed to go home for two weeks out of the year. When you must go that long without seeing your family, you start missing them more than you ever thought you could.

The first time I went home for those precious two weeks, I thought I would melt. The temperature in Alaska when I left was sixty-five degrees below zero before you factored in the wind chill. When I got home, I was greeted with sixty-five-degree temperatures. I saw a few people wearing light jackets, and it made me laugh a little to myself because I felt like it was so hot I could barely breathe. But when I saw Deloris, everything was all right. It was hard to leave and go back north, but my job was not finished yet. I needed to build a new house for her and our son, so I went back to brave the Alaskan wilderness again.

Overall, I had a wonderful time in Valdez, but before long, I found myself boarding yet another plane. The time had come once again to enjoy the sunshine in my native Georgia and to see my family. This time, however, my work was done in Alaska, and I would be going home for good.

I had some good times in Alaska, but I never looked back once I left. The cold, the bears, the unforgiving but beautiful country—all of it was a little too much for this country boy. It had all been worth it, though. As difficult as the work was and as rough as the conditions sometimes were, I ended up making enough to build us a 3,200-square-foot home, as well as save up a nice little nest egg just for such emergencies. I have learned that this life is always going to throw you a curve ball, and it is usually right at the time when you cannot afford it. I had made sure that we would be at least a little more prepared the next time some unforeseen disaster came along. I had left home with little money, worried, feeling somewhat defeated, and unsure if I would even find any work, but God was with me every step of the way and on every plane ride. He saw me through my trials in Alaska, and for that, I will be forever grateful to Him. He never left me, and He never gave up on me, even when there were times I might have given up on myself had it not been for the confidence and strength He gave me to get through it all.

Being home after being away for so long was an amazing feeling. When I was working, I often thought about what it would be like once everything was completed and I was finally home again. So, once I got back, it felt like I was dreaming. Deloris was even more beautiful, warm, caring, and supportive than when I had left. I was reminded then of just how blessed I was to have a woman like her in my life, and throughout the years, I have felt bad for men who do not have wives like mine. I do not see how they face the storms of life without someone who is kind, supportive, and wonderful. She really is an amazing lady, even after all these years. To this day, I often find myself thinking about Proverbs 18:22 (KJV) when I consider just how important she has been in my life. It is a simple verse, but it is just as true now as when it was first written down: "Whoso findeth a wife findeth a good thing, and obtaineth favour of the Lord." Now, when I look back on my life, I feel like I have a little bit of wisdom to impart to others, so if you are a man who is younger than me—and odds are, you probably are—I want you to remember that Bible verse and take it to heart. There is nothing like finding a good woman and building your life with her. On the other hand, there is nothing worse than getting tied up with the wrong woman, so be careful about who you marry. There is no way I would have made it far in life if I'd married a woman who was not as steadfast in her faith, supportive, and loving as Deloris. I am also certain I would not be nearly as happy as I am either.

***

I returned to the warm, sweet air of Georgia early in the year 1977. Like I said earlier, I was on cloud nine after being away for so long. I took a little time off and enjoyed being home, but there was one big problem that soon popped up, and it took a lot of the wind out of my sails. I called around and spoke with the union guys about finding some more work. Though it was a long shot, I inquired specifically about any jobs closer to home since I didn't want to be that far away from my family ever again if I didn't have to. That turned out to be a dream. Those times were dry times for my kind of work in Southeast Georgia, so I had to set my sights further up the country. When that did not work, I figured there might be something out west I could do. No success there, either. Finally, I told them I would be fine with just about any distance they could throw at me, but I kept my fingers crossed that I wouldn't have to go back to Alaska. Well, I did not have to go back to the land of the bears and the mountains of ice and snow, but the best they could get me was Washington State.

The job turned out to be working at a place called the Hanford Reservation, or what they call the Hanford Site today. It was the first large-scale nuclear reactor ever built. If you like history, you might find it interesting to know that the Hanford Reservation was built in 1943 as part of the Manhattan Project. Some of the plutonium there was used in the first nuclear bomb test. Plutonium in the bomb that detonated over Nagasaki, Japan, came from there. Again, it seemed like the ghosts of World War II kept following me. By the time I got there in 1977, they had decommissioned a lot of that stuff and were not using it for weapons anymore. I was not thinking about any of that at the time, though. It was honestly just another job as far as I was concerned, and I was glad to have it.

There I was, far from home again. This time it was only 2,700 miles or so, which was not as far as Alaska. Still, I felt the space between myself and my family even more this time around. I started thinking that being gone that long and being that far from my family again was no way to live, even if the money was good. I have learned that money is a nice thing to have, but it isn't everything. There are some things in life that are not worth sacrificing just to make a dollar. I know a lot of people who work on the road or who do work like I used to do, and it is good, honest work. I also know people whose family lives were put under terrible strains because of that kind of work, and I have known some families that were torn apart by divorces that resulted from working away from home like that for extended periods of time. The money can be particularly good, but sometimes it comes at a great cost. It is not for everybody, that is for sure. To be fair, Deloris and I were not having any problems because of the job, but I knew that I had a good woman and good children. That is more than a lot of men have, and I sure did not want to jeopardize my family life. I also wanted to be around my children more now that they were getting older. So, once I got settled in Washington and found a little apartment to rent, I called Deloris and let her know that this time would be different. We planned to set aside a little money, and I would return for her and my two boys when the time was right. She was overjoyed, and so was I. Looking forward to being together again with my family made me a happy man, and it made me work even harder on the job.

 The nature of my kind of work varies, but I was mostly doing tasks that were similar in one way or another to the kind of work I had done in Alaska. My thoughts were mostly on my family and getting them up there with me so we could be together, but often the nature of the work caused my mind to drift back to the cold, dreary days on the Alaskan pipelines. Even though it had not been that long since I had been up there, it seemed like an entire lifetime had passed. I was glad to have that behind me, but a few things had followed me all the way from Alaska. I am not proud to admit this, and I do not want anyone reading this to follow this example, but it was common for construction workers in those days to start some unhealthy vices. When you are working seven days a week, twelve hours on and twelve hours off, and it is dark outside most of the time with sub-zero temperatures almost everywhere you go, there is not a whole lot to do. You would sleep seven or eight hours out of the twelve hours you had off, then get something to eat right there in the barracks, then go play cards or something else to kill time. Any way you looked at it, there was only so much you could do until you were faced with a crushing sense of boredom. On top of all that, you were out in the middle of nowhere, usually cut off from outside civilization except for the other workers and a small, nearby town. I am sure a lot of the workers there suffered from depression since there was not much sunlight and there was little to do for fun, at least during the hardest cold of the winter months. This is exactly why a lot of us started smoking and drinking. We knew it was not good for us, but it was something to do to pass the time. I was not a big drinker, and I had not smoked much since I had gotten in trouble for cigarettes in high school, but it is plain old human nature to accept that kind of thing when a lot of other people around you are doing it. I would like to tell you that I was strong and resisted those temptations. Unfortunately, I fell victim to the workings of the devil, and I gave in to peer pressure. It was not long before I found myself smoking three packs a day, and I was eventually drinking a pint or more of whiskey each day, as well. Over the course of my life, I have learned that addiction affects us all in one way or another. I have seen and heard of so many people addicted to drugs and alcohol, but the tricky part is that addiction comes in many forms. You can get addicted to a person or the wrong person or to things and situations that are not in themselves bad, but your addiction to them makes them bad because it takes something from your life. It controls you and consumes you. Be careful because it sneaks up on you. When it came to smoking and drinking, I did not even realize I had a problem until God mercifully laid it on my heart. Not many people are that fortunate. I was also lucky in that my vices were the typical combination of alcohol and cigarettes. I thank Almighty God that I have never been a prisoner of drug addiction, but I pray for those who suffer through that and other addictions. Many of them hide it well, and you will never know what they are going through. Some of them may even be close friends or family members. Only God can help those addictions, and I am thankful that He reached down and helped me through mine. May He receive all the glory for helping me overcome it.

Now, He did not just snap His fingers and make me put it down for good. Without His divine help, I could never have done it, but it also took some serious work on my part. If you have ever tried to quit smoking, you know it is not something that most people just walk away from at the drop of a hat. Thanks to the grace of God the Father, I did not find alcohol to be as addictive as cigarettes, though it was still a part of my life. I had backed off on drinking and smoking when I was back in Georgia with my family since I was where I wanted to be, and I did not want to set a bad example for my sons. I had never forgotten how I had grown up and how my dad's alcoholism affected all of us. But once I was back in the routine of working in Washington, the smoking and drinking came back just as strong as ever. It did not help matters that plenty of the other guys I was working with were doing the same things, and there was no one there to tell us to stop or otherwise hold us accountable for our behavior. As far as anybody was concerned, we were free to do whatever we wanted once we were off the clock. Drinking and smoking were not illegal, so they just became part of our routine.

A few months before I left to get Deloris and the kids, God began to work on my heart concerning my vices. Stubbornly, I resisted. I felt a kind of nagging in my mind about what I was doing, but I brushed it off. I have not always been the man of God that I am today, and I sure would not ever claim to be perfect. During this time, God had not yet directly called me into His service, so I was going along with my life, doing what I thought was normal. He kept working with me, though, and He finally put it in my mind to give up the cigarettes and whiskey for good. Those were hard things to let go of, especially the cigarettes. It would not be long before I would get a, sure enough, wake-up call from the Creator Himself, but that would not happen until I had brought my family up to Washington to be with me full-time.

***

When it comes to quitting cigarettes, they tell you the first three days or so are the toughest. In my experience, it was more like three months. I do not know if quitting drinking at the same time had something to do with it, but my nerves were completely shot. I could not think straight, and I was angry all the time. Any little comment, thought, or inconvenience would set me off, and I would have to take several deep breaths and realize why I was feeling that way. I kept thinking that everything would be worth it once I got through the roughest part of my nicotine and alcohol withdrawals. We did not have nicotine patches or gum or anything like that back then, so I had to do it all cold turkey.

I brought my family back up from Georgia during the toughest part of it all. Deloris could see what I was going through, and she kept telling the kids to stop talking so much since I was trying to quit smoking. I knew I was in a bad mood, and knowing I was in a bad mood seemed to put me in an even worse mood, but I hunkered down, gripped the steering wheel, and focused on driving to try and keep my cravings out of my mind. Somehow, we made it back up to Washington in one piece, and I did not have any true outbursts along the way. It is with immense joy in my heart that I can honestly say I haven't smoked a cigarette or consumed a drop of alcohol since 1977. The Father helped me tremendously, as did my wife and children. Deloris supported me through it all, just as she always has, and having her and the kids there in Washington served as a constant reminder of why I was trying to quit. I wanted to be around all of them for as long as I could, and I knew that smoking and drinking would later bring on a slew of health problems. I was sometimes reminded of my dad, as well. I was never angry or violent when I drank, but it did not matter. I did not want my children to grow up with a dad that went through a pint of whiskey a day. I wanted to be a man my wife and kids could be proud of, and I finally realized that drinking and smoking were not for me because my life was headed in a new direction, and I wanted to wipe it all out of my life and set a better example for my family.

Three packs of cigarettes a day is a lot of smoking, but I quit. Praise the Lord! Looking back on that victory over those vices, I realize that Satan had come against me once again. That old tempter is sneaky. He crept up on me and started taking control before I even knew what happened, but God once again said, "No!" and commanded the devil to take his hand from me. It has been that way throughout my whole life. Just when Satan and his forces had the upper hand, God spared my family and me. I have learned many things from my long life and from communing with God, but one of the most important things is that Satan will never be the ultimate victor over any of God's children. Jesus knew this, of course, and that is why He said in John 10:10 (KJV) that "I am come that they might have life, and that they might have it more abundantly." This works in many ways, figuratively and literally, but in my case, He helped me to have a more abundant life as far as my health was concerned. There is no telling how many years I would have cut off of my life had I not quit my addictions, and I'm so glad He's seen fit to keep me healthy, mobile, and happy even now that I'm eighty years old. Even after those years of abusing my body, I have nothing physically wrong with me at all. I do not know many people my age who can say the same thing, and I thank Him every day for these blessings upon me. As amazing as His help was in crushing my addictions, that was nothing compared to how He was about to work in my life shortly afterward.

***

I do not know of many people who have ever experienced what I did on that special day in 1977.

What I am about to tell you may seem farfetched, especially if you are not a believer. You need to know that I was indeed sober and was not under the influence of any drugs of any kind. What happened next is the truth, just as I lived it.

This was before I had brought Deloris and the kids up to live with me, so I was still renting a small apartment in Washington, staying right by myself.

I was in my bedroom one evening, praying to God as I was trying to draw myself closer to Him. I had already seen the miracles He had worked in my life so many times, and I felt a fervent desire to have a more personal relationship with Him. It was as if He was pulling me closer to Him, and I finally felt ready to go wherever He might lead me. During my prayers, the phone rang. I was a little disappointed since this time in prayer was a serious thing to me even then, and I guarded that time as much as I could. Reluctantly, I went to the phone and picked it up. My sister-in-law answered from way back home in Georgia. Now, she had called to check up on me from time to time, but this call just felt different from the moment I picked up the telephone. Her voice was different somehow, and she seemed like she was on an important mission. We did not spend much time doing the usual chit-chat. Instead, she got right down to the point: she had called because she had felt led by the Lord to pray with me. I appreciated it, and while I had no clue what she was going to pray about, I went along with it. When I had taken her call, I felt just a little disappointed to have my own prayer time interrupted, but all of that left my mind almost immediately. She prayed with me for just a little while before she began to speak in tongues. Speaking in tongues is a special thing to me. I know not every Christian denomination believes in it, while some do, even though they might not understand it. Many have never experienced it. If you do not know what I am talking about, speaking in tongues basically means that God speaks through you. You say things that sound like a language, but the words are not translatable with any dictionary. It is more about God working through you and working through the person or the people hearing you. He leads you to the interpretation He wants you to have. This has been done since biblical times, and you usually see it practiced among Pentecostal Christian denominations. There has been controversy about it for years and years, but I am here to tell you it is real. I have experienced it myself many times, but never the way I experienced it that evening.

My sister-in-law was moved by the Spirit of God when His Spirit was poured out from on high. I am sure of that. It was more powerful than anything I had felt up to that point. The interpretation rendered to me said that God was going to do remarkable things in my life. He said, "I will make this covenant with you. I am going to heal you physically and financially. You have work to do for Me. Just show up, and I'll send the people."

Let me tell you something. When you receive a message like that, you do not have to wonder about who it came from. The presence of the Almighty filled that room on that day like fire. To say I was shocked was an understatement for sure. I knew what He was saying to me, but I was confused. What did He want me to do, exactly? There was not anything physically wrong with me at that point. In fact, He had just helped me to give up smoking and drinking for good. What did He mean by healing me financially? I was doing okay with the job on the Hanford Reservation. It did not make much sense. What really puzzled me was the part about Him sending the people if I just showed up. When you get a message from God that tells you to show up, you'd better show up! I wanted to do as He asked, but I did not know where to start.

I finished the call with my sister-in-law and hung up. I did not ask her any of these questions because I knew she would not have the answers. She was just bringing me the message, and it was up to me to decipher God's will. It is amazing how a person's life can change so suddenly. One minute I was going about my day, working my job, and praying. In the span of just a few minutes, I was now faced with trying to understand a very real and serious plan that the Creator of all things had commanded of me. I am no prophet, and I am not a perfect man. I am nobody special, but for some reason, God saw fit to work directly in my life. It sure put things in perspective in a hurry, and I felt a huge sense of responsibility to do His will.

All of this weighed heavily on my mind for the rest of that day. It did not feel like a burden at all. Instead, it felt like an exciting mission, and it gave me a powerful sense of purpose and meaning in my life because this was not about me—it was all about Him. I wanted to be of service in any way I could.

By the time I went to bed that night, I figured the Father had intended for me to become a preacher or to work in the ministry in some way. That seemed like the most direct and obvious choice.

Before I climbed into bed, though, I decided to pray about it. I knew God could see what was on my heart and in my mind, but I wanted to bring it before Him and ask Him if I was on the right track. I prayed and prayed, asking my Holy Father if He wanted me to preach for Him. I waited a long time but felt nothing. Now, the human mind is good at understanding many things, but when it comes to serious matters like the ones I was dealing with, I have found that discernment from God often comes in the form of a feeling. It is a lot like faith itself. You can study it all you want, but part of it will always be a feeling or a movement of your soul. It is difficult to explain, but if you have ever felt it, you know what I mean. I continued to feel absolutely nothing but not an emptiness. It was as if He was telling me, "Try again."

By this point, I had gotten into bed. I started praying again, and this time I asked God if He had special work for me to do other than preaching. To me, preaching is an incredibly important activity in the service of God. I thought that if it was something other than that, it must be truly special.

What follows is hard to believe, but it is the truth. I lived it, and it still amazes me to this day. I know that I had not gone to sleep yet, so it was not a dream. I felt something on the center of my back suddenly, but for some reason, I was not afraid. The hairs on my arms stood on end, and goosebumps popped up all over me. It was like the hand of God Himself. Gently, slowly, He lifted me straight up off the bed. My head and heels remained on the bed. Once He had raised me up, He slowly brought me back down to rest on my bed. He did this three times, and each time was the same. It was a measured, controlled, caring sort of movement, like the way you would lift a scared child before you hold him tight to you and tell him everything will be all right. The presence of the Holy Spirit filled the room when He laid me down for the last time, and I remained there.

I could not move. I could not talk. I wondered if I was dead, but I blinked a few times and turned my head, astonished. I waited for Him to do or say something else, but He did not. I expected to lie there all night after what I had just experienced, but He knew what was on my mind. He saw fit to allow me to drift into a deep, restful sleep within just a few minutes.

Chapter 5

Once I had my family with me in Washington, I was overjoyed. Now that I was nicotine and alcohol-free, I felt so much better at work, and it was exciting for me to get off work and go back to the apartment to see Deloris and the kids. It renewed our family life, and it made me a much happier man. The work at the Hanford Reservation could be tough and stressful, but all of that melted away when I saw my family each day.

As happy as I was, it was all short-lived.

Work slowed down again, and before long, I found myself laid off. That is the nature of this kind of work, unfortunately. You know it is coming eventually, but it does not make the situation any easier when the work ends. It always seemed to happen just when things were on the upswing, too. I had been through worse, and I knew that God would help me, Deloris, and the kids through it yet again. I found work with a friend of mine at a paper mill five and a half hours away in Mazola, Montana. Unfortunately, this meant I would have to leave my family once again. I was worried I might start back drinking and smoking again without my family around, but God did not fail me. I had plenty of chances to give in to those temptations, but He kept me strong against them. Deloris and the kids stayed on in Washington until the paper mill job was completed, then I returned for them. We temporarily settled in Kennewick, Washington, which was a little less than twenty miles from the Hanford Reservation.

I was glad to be back in Washington with my family, but it took several weeks before I found more work. I ended up heading back to the Hanford Reservation to work at the powerhouse. Thankfully, that lasted until 1980. By that time, I decided it was time to head to Georgia. I had heard through the grapevine that work was picking up closer to home, so Deloris and I packed up the kids and pointed my truck toward home.

***

Washington State had been good to us. While it was not home, the weather was not nearly as brutal, and I had the chance to keep my family close by. Most importantly, however, God had worked in my life in an astonishing way. Through it all, I kept trying to understand what it was He wanted me to do. I prayed, and I looked for signs that He might send me—anything that might bring me a little closer to understanding His plan for my life. I received nothing in the way of guidance, so I kept on with work and decided that He would open my eyes regarding those matters only when the time was right.

As much as I had enjoyed my time in Washington, it was good to be home in Georgia again. Once we had gotten settled back into our house, I called up the union hall and went straight back to work. Things really were picking up again in the Peach State.

Everything was going better than I could have imagined until I started hurting. This pain came over me out of nowhere, and it would not leave me alone. The nagging pain continued, and it intensified over the course of the next two weeks until I was a total wreck. I remember lying on the couch in our living room, thinking I would take a nap and feel a little better when I woke up. That did not work out at all.

As much as I needed the rest, I could not get any sleep. I was wracked with pain, tossing and turning, unable to find any relief. I was weak all over, but I stood up and saw that I had cracked the imitation leather on the couch from my twisting and turning. Before long, I felt a twinge in my stomach and rushed into the bathroom to throw up. I knelt over the toilet after vomiting, and the pain overtook me to the point that I broke down and cried. I had been sick before, but I had never experienced anything like this. I could not think straight, eat, or do much of anything except writhe in pain. To be honest, I thought I was going to die.

Deloris tried to help me, but there was nothing she could do. It tore her up inside to see me like that and not be able to do anything to help me. The next day, she called up the doctor and told him what was going on with me. He simply replied that it could be anything and instructed her not to let me lie there. According to him, it was possible that I might die if I did not get to a hospital as soon as possible.

The searing pain was so bad that I do not remember much of the ride there or much of what happened afterward. I was so focused on the pain that I only vaguely understood that they were taking X-rays. After that, Deloris comforted me as I sat doubled over in my chair, waiting for the doctor to come out and give us the news about what was wrong with me. At that point, I did not care much about what the doctor said. I just wanted to know what was causing this excruciating pain and how to fix it.

It turned out that all of this was caused by two large kidney stones. They were so big that the doctor said it would take surgery to remove them. Well, at least I knew what was going on. We scheduled the surgery, but I felt like I would not be able to last that long. Every muscle in my body had been on edge for so long that I was completely exhausted all the time, though I could not sleep a wink due to the non-stop pain. They gave me some morphine pills to give me some relief until they could get me in for the surgery, then sent us home.

On the ride home, my first thought was to pop open that bottle and get those pills working in my system. But then it occurred to me that this was not what I needed to do. It was the first truly clear thought I'd had since the pain had set in. I thought back to what God had told me back in Washington about how He was going to heal me physically and financially. Back then, I was in decent shape, so it didn't make much sense. But once the kidney stones had caused that debilitating pain, I saw it as the fulfillment of what He was trying to tell me. I have learned that God communicates with people in His own way, and you have to do a little work of your own and have a lot of faith in what He says or does in your life. Oftentimes what He is trying to get across to you will not make sense until the time is right.

Deloris drove as smoothly and as quickly as she could, making sure not to hit any bumps in the road that might jostle me around and cause me any more pain. Once we were home, she helped me inside and was about to get ready to give me some of the morphine pills. I set the bottle on the counter and told God that I trusted Him. If it were His will, I would die before I took any of that medicine. Now, understand that I am not against taking medicine. Plenty of people need it to live healthy, fulfilled lives, and I do not begrudge them for it. But at that time, in that situation, taking those pills would have meant that I did not trust in God. I could have popped one of those things, got some relief, and crawled into my bed for some well-deserved rest. Instead, I believed in what He had told me back in Washington, and if I needed to suffer through this affliction to prove my faith and trust in Him, then I would gladly do it.

I explained what I was doing to Deloris, and she understood. As much as she would have liked to have seen me get some relief before the surgery, she supported my decision, and we trusted in the Lord to make it right, just as He had said He would. She helped me to bed and prayed fervently to the Father. I was in agony, and my thoughts were all jumbled to the point that it was hard just to pray, but I focused hard and reminded Him that He had promised to physically heal me. I remember being so desperate that I asked Him why He had not healed me yet. It did not make any sense to me. I had trusted in Him, and He continued to let me suffer. Despite all the pain, I somehow drifted off to sleep.

Before I knew what was happening, the Almighty immediately impressed upon my heart the very reason He had not chosen to heal me. I did not even realize it until He brought it to my attention, but He showed me that I harbored a dislike for a family member. I will not go into details about who this person was, but suffice it to say, this person was doing some things with which I did not agree. It was not anything horrible, but I saw that these activities would lead that person nowhere fast. There was no outright hatred in my heart for this family member, just a dislike. These ill feelings for my family member created an obstacle for me that I had never thought of before. Amazed that God had shown me the true workings of my own heart, I promised Him that I would make it right with this family member if He would follow through on what He had told me and deliver me from this physical pain.

Let this be a lesson to you. Even when you think you are living right and following God's plan, it is all too easy to let things such as resentment and dislike creep into your mind and into your heart. The worst part about all of this is that you are often unaware of it. Thankfully, the Lord pointed this out to me so that I could work on it and become a person better fit to serve Him eventually. He had plans for me, and He was not about to proceed with those plans until I had cleaned out every scrap of that dislike I had developed for my family member.

As soon as I told Him that I would make it right with this person, I fell into a deep, restful sleep. I awoke the next day and sat up in bed, but I felt strange. It took a moment for me to realize what it was—for the first time in two weeks, I had absolutely no pain! I had grown so accustomed to the pain that being without it felt odd. My muscles were still weak, but I got up out of bed and made it to the bathroom on my own. I was relieved to find that I could once again urinate without any problems. He had healed me, just as He had said He would. Praise God!

If you have ever suffered from kidney stones—especially ones as large as mine were—you know how sweet it is to finally have relief from them. The first thing I did was tell Deloris about my miraculous recovery. Doctor Jesus had healed me faster and more fully than any mortal doctor ever could—all because I believed in Him and trusted Him to do what He had promised. It was not until many years later that I found out what had happened. One of the kidney stones in my bladder had vanished overnight, while the other stayed, although it has never caused me any more pain to this day.

Just as I thought everything was about to go back to normal, my doctor ordered me to abstain from all forms of sweets. He said that sweets could cause me to have a buildup of gas and lots of pain because of what I had gone through with the kidney stones. I did not think much of it, and I had more or less forgotten about it by the time I got home. All I was thinking about was how great it felt to be rid of that awful pain and how amazing it was to know that my Creator had reached down and performed a miracle for a regular, undeserving person like me.

I had never been one to pig out on sweets, but something about knowing you are not supposed to have something has a way of making you want it that much more. It did not take long for me to set my eyes on a chocolate pie in the refrigerator back home. Any other time, I would have glanced over it without much thought, but it was all I could think about over the next few days. I kept hearing the doctor's orders in my head, and I knew I should not so much as touch that pie, but the temptation kept building. It really was silly, and I felt like a little kid, but I could not help it. I waited until Deloris was not around for a little while, then I snatched that pie out of the refrigerator, grabbed a fork and a plate, and set down to eat it on the kitchen counter as if I had never had pie in my whole life. I thought I would have a slice or two, then stop for the day. Deloris would fuss at me for going against the doctor's orders, but at least I would have gotten the pie craving out of my system. Well, that is not at all what happened. Once I started, I did not stop until all I could see was the bottom of the pie pan. A few crumbs sat on the plate and clung to my fork as the only evidence that the pie had ever existed at all. That was some good eating.

As soon as I had finished, I felt guilty. I started getting paranoid, expecting the stomach pains the doctor had warned me about. I waited and waited, but nothing ever happened. This was not a little pie either, so I thought that if any sweets were going to hurt me, it would be that pie. No pain ever came over me because of eating it, and I was once again amazed. Now, I should not have gone against my doctor's orders in the first place, and I did not have any more cravings like that again, but to think that I was still fine was proof to me that it is best to believe in God's report. It was His way of showing me that He was in control and that He would continue to take care of me. God healed me from my kidney stones, and He healed me from any problems from eating those sweets. It reminded me of Isaiah 53:5 (KJV), "He was wounded for our transgressions, he was bruised for our iniquities: the chastisement of our peace was upon him; and with his stripes we are healed." I was healed then and have been healed so many times over by the stripes of Jesus Christ. Praise God!

***

The kidney stones had brought me as low as I had ever been up to that point in my life, at least physically. Overcoming them through the help of God the Father had given me a new lease on life, and ever since that day, I have reminded myself of how important it is to have and maintain good health. Thankfully, the Lord has seen fit to bless me with excellent health to this day.

One of the worst things about being in poor health is that you cannot live a full life—you cannot be there for your family, you cannot enjoy the things you like to do, and you sure cannot make much money if you are in terrible pain all the time. I had been laid up for two whole weeks, and during that time, the last thing on my mind was looking for work. I would not have been much use on a job site at that point, anywhere.

Now that I was feeling good again, I jumped out there and called up the union hall. I half-expected them to tell me they did not have anything for me or that they had some work that was hundreds, if not thousands, of miles away. To my surprise, they set me up with a job at a paper mill that was only about a forty-five-minute drive from Waycross. I would be able to see my family on a regular basis without having to drag them across the country with me. The town where the paper mill was located is a good small town, and I should know since, years later, I would settle for good not far from there. It is smaller in size than Waycross, but it is still one of those ideal small towns like you see in the movies. Everybody knows everybody, things move at a slow, easy pace, and you never feel overwhelmed with lots of people.

This mill was the place to be, and I was happy to work there. It was a good thing to be a part of. It was bittersweet, however, since it was not long before they transferred me down to Florida to work at another mill owned by the same company. That mill was only about an hour and a half away from my home, so the distance was not that bad. I stayed there for almost a year. During that time, they promoted me to the level of supervisor. Once again, things were looking up for this country boy.

After the year was up, I got to come back to the mill close to Waycross, where I stayed from 1980 to 1988. Getting to stay close to Waycross and have stable work for all that time truly was a blessing to my family and me, and I thank God for it still. Had I needed to, I would have gladly shipped off all across the country to provide for Deloris and the kids, but I wouldn't have enjoyed it. It sure was a nice eight years, and I still look back on that time fondly. In 1988, though, I had to head up to a facility located in Southeast Georgia, which was about an hour and a half from my home in Waycross. I did not think much of it at the time, but I would soon find out that this job would test my patience and my skills in ways I'd never encountered.

This job in Southeast Georgia was an amazing industrial plant and a unique place to work. The previous contractor had not finished the job—he had installed a polymer line, but it was not working. It was a simple, in-and-out job that would not take too long to accomplish. All we had to do was clean up somebody else's mess, which happens sometimes. Some contractors are full of big talk, but once they get out there on the job, they cannot see things through. That is when it takes a crew who knows what they're doing to make it happen. I have always taken considerable pride in my work, and I want to leave a job knowing that it's done. There is no sense in leaving a mess for someone else to clean up.

Now that I was a foreman with a mechanic and an apprentice to help me, I thought it would be a breeze. Well, it did not take long for us to figure out we had grabbed a tiger by the tail with this one.

I had never seen anything like it. We thought it was just a polymer line that needed fixing, but we were faced with a rat's nest of wires, sometimes leading off in no direction and looping back on themselves other times. Even when this kind of work is done correctly, it is difficult to know what is doing what and which wires are going where. That is why the wires are always color-coded and labeled. You never know when one of them might need to be replaced. These wires, however, were missing most of their labels and numbering schematics. Even the color coding did not help us much. We looked over the site, and all of us looked at each other with dismay. This seemed like an impossible task. Instead of looking for a needle in a haystack, we had to find hundreds of needles in hundreds of haystacks. We knew what we were up against, but there was not any other choice—we had signed on for the job, and we were going to see it through.

No matter how much gumption and determination we had, there was one piece of the puzzle that turned out to be our redeeming feature on that impossible job: an old printer in one of the plant's offices. Now that we had a printer, we could at least trace the wires, track where they were going to and where they were supposed to go, and take inventory of what was working and what was not. It was painstaking, meticulous work, but we got to it, using the printer to create makeshift labels for each wire in that place. Once we were done, we loaded up and got out of there. All of us were sick of seeing those wires, and I would not have been surprised if I had caught myself labeling and tracing wires in my sleep!

I headed back to the mill in Georgia, but before long, the man I was working for called me. At first, I was worried that we had done something wrong at that industrial plant. I went over it all in my head, but I could not think of a single thing we had left out. To my pleasant surprise, he told me to get everything together and go back over there for more work. It turns out that the other contractor had left long before completing several other jobs there. I told him I would be glad to go back since it was a huge opportunity for all of us. I have learned that if you keep doing great work and earn a good reputation for your work ethic, it won't be too long before somebody notices and gives you a chance. I do not recall who the other contractor was that left, but I owe him a lot. Had he done his job, I might not have had the chance and success that I did. God was there for me once again, making a way for me even when I was not aware of it. To tell the truth, I was doing fine where I was. Even so, this new opportunity is one I jumped on without hesitation.

When I got there, it turned out that those "several jobs" amounted to over a year or so of solid work. I was overjoyed and thanked God for this latest blessing in my life. We worked diligently for about a year there before I got another call unexpectedly. It was the general contractor over the whole thing. He asked me if I would be interested in securing my own electrical contractor's license from the state of Georgia. He had been keeping a close eye on me for a while and wanted me to go into business with him.

I was floored. I thought back to working in Alaska, and how rough it was out there, and how far away from my family I had to go just to get that work. The pay had been great at the time, and I had been grateful for it, but if this went through, it would be a life-changing financial move for me. With the help of God the Father, I had certainly come a long way.

***

I agreed to get my license, and the general contractor was pleased. It had been a long time since I'd studied for a test, but Deloris was there for me. She hit the books right along with me, and we used every spare minute to work in some study sessions. I had passed the test to get into the union, so I knew I could do this. Even so, this was altogether different compared to the test to get into the union, and I was nervous about it. So much was riding on passing this one test, and I could see it all either coming together or slipping out of my fingers. After a few months, I was about burned out with all of that studying, especially since I was still working and making it a point to spend quality time with my family. It seemed like there was no more studying to be done at that point, so I decided to go in and give it a shot. I felt confident but ended up failing the exam by five measly points. Failing that exam stung, but I knew I could pass it since it was only a matter of five points. Deloris and I took to studying yet again, this time with a renewed drive. This time, I had to make it happen.

After a few more months of studying, I was ready to go back in and retake the test. Deloris believed in me and even told me that she would tie balloons all over my truck in celebration if I passed the exam. I cannot stress enough how important it has been for me to have her in my life. She has been there for me through the ups and downs and all the successes and failures. Deloris' confidence bolstered my own spirits, and I knew that somehow, someway, God was working in my life, even if I did not pass the exam.

When I got there to take the test, I was surprised to see several of the guys who had been there when I took the test the first time around. They called each other by name, laughed, and cut up like they were old friends. I asked them what was going on, and they told me that they had not been on jobs together in the past, nor were they exactly close friends with each other. Instead, they knew one another from taking this test two and even three times. Several of these guys were much younger than me, and some of them were even still in college. At least one of them was at that time attending a well-known university in Georgia. I had walked in, brimming with confidence, but at that moment, my heart sank. I was not cut out for this, after all. These men were much more highly educated than I was, so how did I expect to pass this exam? Despite the multitude of blessings God had bestowed upon me, I still doubted myself and my abilities. I should not have felt that way, but I did. That is only human. Remember, though, that God is with you, and He will make a way for you if you only follow Him and do as He commands of you.

I knew it would take a little while to get the results back, but I tried not to think about it and focused instead on the job back at the industrial plant. One day soon afterward, one of the guys on the job came to me and asked if my wife was going to have another baby. I cannot remember exactly what I was doing at the time, but it caught me off guard. Stunned, I stopped what I was doing and just looked at him for a moment. "No," I replied. He could easily see how puzzled I was. "Why would you ask me that?" I continued.

"Well," he said, "I just happened to look over at your truck a few minutes ago when I was in the parking lot."

"Yeah?" I asked.

"Somebody's put balloons all over it."

I grinned, and it was his turn to look a little confused.

I rushed outside, and sure enough, Deloris had tied at least a dozen balloons onto my truck. I headed to the nearest phone in the plant and called Deloris at home. She told me she had gotten the call earlier that day, explaining that I had indeed passed the test. She had driven all the way to my workplace and covered my truck with balloons as a little surprise. Once again, I had beaten the odds. I might have had to leave high school before graduating, and I may never have been a straight-A student, but I had just passed one of the most important tests of my life—and I could not have done it without her support. Little did I know that I would be challenged with many more tests over the years, and not the kind you pass or fail using a pen and paper. At that moment, however, all I could think about was how good it felt to achieve something that I had wanted so badly and had worked so hard for. God had helped me through it yet again.

Passing the exam meant that I could now apply for my electrical contractor's license and go into business with the general contractor I had been working through. I had never owned a business before, so the prospect of starting one from scratch was overwhelming. Then again, I had taken on plenty of challenges in my life up to that point. Many times, I had gone after goals that required me to learn new skills along the way, so I looked at this next venture as a challenge that I would figure out. As always, I knew that these blessings were coming from the Lord, and He was not about to leave me high and dry after opening so many doors for me. It was especially exciting since this was a challenge that I wanted and not one that was thrust upon me. Now I had reached a point in my life in which I was no longer trying to claw my way out of a tough situation. Instead, this was an opportunity to move up in the world, make a lot more money, tithe more, and be able to take even better care of my family.

My dad's old refrain of "You'll never make anything out of yourself" was about as faint as it could be. I might have been born just a simple country boy, but I was about to become a legitimate business owner, doing something I knew a lot about. I hope this shows you that you do not have to be some big shot or a special person for God to work in your life. The Bible is filled with stories of ordinary people who were brought into the service of God and who received His blessings. He is still doing the same things today as He always has, even if people do not like to admit it or pay attention to it. I am living proof of this, and you do not have to look far to find other examples of it. Glory be to God!

Chapter 6

I started my own electrical contracting company in 1990. It is funny to think about it now, but we only had two employees at the time. You must start somewhere, and my company was no different. One of the employees was an Inside Journeyman Wireman, and the other was an apprentice. I continued working under the same general contractor, although I was technically working with him through my own company. Right from the start, I decided it would be best to be a union contractor, although the other contractor on the job was non-union. Things rolled along smoothly for a few years, but then the non-union contractor passed away.

My company began picking up extra work during that time. The increased revenue meant we could hire more people and expand our operations. We ended up hiring another foreman, two more journeymen, and two extra apprentices. Now, you might think that Deloris and I were rolling in money along that time. I sure thought that was how it would go, but that certainly was not the case. At the time, we were living in a twenty-eight-foot travel trailer that served as our home and office. Sounds glamorous, doesn't it? Although my company was generating more revenue than ever, most of it was going out the door to pay for all the costs of doing business. We had to pay our employees, pay taxes, and all the other overhead and expenses. We hired a good accountant to help with the finances. He helped us to write off all that we could and legally save as much as we could, but there just was not that much left over for us. Even then, I was only getting paid every thirty to forty-five days out of the company's profits, and some weeks I did not even receive a check because there was nothing left over. They do not tell you all this when you go into business for yourself, and this is why a lot of people either don't start a business or get out of it soon after getting everything off the ground. It was tough, but we hung in there, knowing that if we just held on, we would be better off for it. Neither of us had been well-off when we were younger, so we knew how to cope with those hard financial times. Unlike those days back when we first got married, we could see the light at the end of the tunnel.

Within three or four years of scraping by like this, we made enough from the company to purchase a double-wide mobile home. This was a big upgrade from the little travel trailer, and it felt more like a real home to us.

It took five long years before my accountant showed me all our books and said it was time for me to begin taking a weekly paycheck out of my company. It was not much at the time, but it was steady and dependable. During those five years, I wondered if I had made the right decision or misinterpreted the situation. I should have just stuck with what I was doing. Despite those doubts, I stayed the course, and God saw me through it. Those regular paychecks grew little by little, but we still barely had enough to pay our bills. After five years of tightening our belts when it came to money, I was discouraged. This is what being a business owner was all about? This is what I had waited for? It did not make much sense.

About that time, the general contractor who had put all this in motion called me. He was pleased with our business arrangement, but he had decided to pursue other things. At first, I thought that he was leaving our partnership, but what he wanted was something better than I could have imagined. He wanted to sell his portion of the company to me. This was an amazing opportunity since I could do things the way I wanted to do them. I had socked away a good amount into savings, and I worked some things around to be able to afford it, but we went through with the deal. After it was done, my company really took off. We started making more money, and suddenly we could pay our bills with ease and have a little left over each month. Finally, we arrived at a situation in which we could pay all our employees, keep the company running, and keep a good bit for ourselves. Yet again, things turned around just when it seemed the darkest. God had made a way for me, just like He always had.

It occurred to me then that God had made good on His promise. All this time, I had often wondered what His plan for me might be. Once again, I did not think I even needed to be healed financially since I was doing okay with my jobs. But He had come through for me by not only giving me the opportunity to start my own company, but He saw me through those first five rough years. Since then, my company has had some difficulties but has continued to thrive through it all. I am glad to say that I do not have to worry about money today. Money is not everything, and you certainly cannot buy your way into heaven with it, but it gives you so much confidence and security when you know you do not have to worry about where your next meal or your next job is coming from. Looking back on my entire career, I owe every penny I have ever made to the Lord. Therefore, I have never stopped tithing since Deloris convinced me that it was the right thing to do—none of it really belongs to me, anyway. He blesses me the more I give back to Him, and you cannot outgive God. Later, I would go beyond tithing, but that would not be until God finally showed me what He wanted me to do in His service. He engineered everything perfectly because if all these things had not happened in exactly the way they did, in that exact order, I would never have been able to do the work He would later call me to do.

Now that I realized all of what He had done for me, it was clear—God had physically healed me in 1980, and He had done the same for me financially in 1990. It had all been worth it, and I was excited to see where this new chapter of my life would take my family and me. If God were at the helm—as I knew He was—everything would be okay. All I had to do was keep on doing the best that I could, and He would throw light on the remaining mysteries of His covenant to me when the time was right.

* * *

There were very few buildings at the plant back in 1990. Early on, my company was given a job that included various electrical installations at a facility close to home. We were involved with the installation of switchgear and all the control cabinets that went along with it. We wired the warehouse, overhead lighting, power ramps, and several docks. This was a huge undertaking, and we did a jam-up job on all of it, which bolstered the reputation of my company even more.

The next year saw even more jobs for my company. The work continued to roll in at a rapid pace. We were given more projects, and in 1992 we took on more work at another location not too far from Savannah, Georgia. This involved working at an industrial facility. The work kept rolling in. In 1993, we acquired more jobs and all the electrical work at another facility, which was not that difficult since it was nearly identical to the work, we'd done just a year before. I was amazed at what God had provided for my company. Within just three years, we had already accomplished so much and had been given jobs that bigger, more established companies would usually take over. Also, in 1993, we worked on a maintenance building, emergency generators, and air compressors. I could go on and on with God's blessings on my company, but suffice it to say that this much activity was unusual for a company that had not been around all that long. As I have said before, I take considerable pride in my work and the work that is done by my employees. I have made it a point to surround myself with good people in my personal life, and the same goes for my professional life as well. My company's reputation has been rock solid since day one because of this, but it was the Father who opened so many doors for us in those first few critical years. He continues to do so today.

It is important to remember that the Lord has never promised us that our walk with Him would be easy. My life has been a testament to His grace, mercy, power, and amazing love, but you will notice that all of these blessings and victories have been mixed with health issues, financial troubles, and potential death at times. What happened next was another one of those low points, and I am certain that Satan was behind it all. You see, Satan cannot stand to see someone doing right in the eyes of God, and he sure will not sit idly by while the Lord continues to bless you. Whenever you are going through those rough times, always remember that God has His hand over you.

One day in 1993, I was going about my business as usual. I was at work when I started to feel bad. It was nothing like what I had experienced with those two huge kidney stones, but I felt rough, nonetheless. Since I am not prone to sickness, this was an unusual feeling, and I brushed it aside, thinking that maybe I was just coming down with a cold. I figured I might eat some soup that night and get in bed early to head it off, and everything would be fine the next day. Well, it did not take long before I started feeling so bad that I ended up leaving work. I had been pushing myself hard along that time and was glad to do so since everything was coming together with my company, but I thought I just needed some rest.

On the drive home, though, I felt even worse. I could not figure out what was wrong with me, and it had me worried. I arrived home and took to the couch, thinking that a little rest would not hurt, whether it was a cold or just exhaustion from working so hard. I had just settled in on the couch when I sat upright and felt a sneeze coming on. I held the back of my hand up to my nose and sneezed hard. When I did, I felt something wet all over my hand. At first, I thought about how inconvenient it would be to get up and go to the bathroom for some tissue to wipe my hand, but when I opened my eyes after sneezing, I could not believe what I saw. The back of my hand was spattered all over with blood. When I looked down to see if I had gotten any on my shirt, I saw that my nose was pouring blood. I jumped up and ran for the bathroom, stringing blood on the carpet all the way. The bathroom sink, the floor, and the toilet ended up covered in my blood. All I could think to do was to stuff some toilet paper into my nostrils and hold my head back. That did not work because I was bleeding too much and far too fast. I hung my head over the sink and ran the water from the faucet. All I could do was watch the blood continue to pour from my nose and wash down the sink. This kept on for quite some time, and I was scared. This was no regular nosebleed. I have never been afraid of the sight of blood, but this was too much. I was worried I might bleed out, but it finally let up, and I went to bed, puzzled about whatever was happening to my body.

The next day, I went straight to my doctor. I had managed to stop the bleeding, but I was concerned that it might come back at any time. What really upset me was the fact that I had no idea what the underlying cause might be. I still felt bad all over, but I could not put my finger on it. It was just a general feeling of being unwell, much different from any kind of sickness I had ever dealt with. My doctor took me back into the examination room and did some tests on me, then left for a little while. I waited for him to come back with the news about my condition, and it felt like he was gone for hours. My mind raced to the worst possible outcomes, but I took a deep breath and tried to calm myself. Whatever it was, I hoped it was not some serious, debilitating, lifelong illness. If something knocked me out of the saddle now, I would be finished. I had always prided myself on being a good husband and father, and the thought of becoming a burden to them was unbearable.

When the doctor finally came back, he gave me a look of surprise. This, obviously, was not what I was expecting at all. He said that my blood pressure was 195 over 165. I am no doctor, but even I know that's dangerously high. He went on to explain that this would have normally caused me to have a stroke, but something quite interesting and unusual had occurred instead. His tests revealed that I had suffered an aneurysm. While this was supposed to have killed me, the burst blood vessel did not create lethal pressure inside my head the way it normally would. Instead, my forceful sneeze acted like a pressure relief valve. In his estimation, I could have very easily died had I not sneezed at that exact time and with that much force. I grinned and nodded my head. I silently thanked God because I knew that Satan had once again tried to kill me, but God stood in his way and saved me. He had said, "No!" on my behalf in the face of my destroyer.

As always, I did not get out of that situation scot-free. My blood pressure was still through the roof, and my doctor said that I would be in some real trouble quite soon if I did not get it down to a more manageable and healthy level. He wrote me a prescription for forty milligrams of blood pressure medication. I struggled with this for a little bit since God had healed me before when I'd had kidney stones. However, I had a good feeling about this medication, as though He was telling me to go ahead and take it. So, I took the medicine, but I wanted to go a step further. Although I was no stranger to working hard, I knew I was not in the best shape. If I wanted to be around for a long time for my wife and children, I knew I needed to start exercising regularly. In turn, this would go a long way toward lowering my blood pressure and keeping it at a safe level.

Boy, am I glad I decided to make exercise an integral part of my life. My weight dropped from 204 pounds down to 154 pounds in no time. I am not a large man with a big frame, so staying around 150 pounds was great for me. Before long, my doctor cut my prescription in half since my exercise regimen had naturally brought my blood pressure down. Today, I do not take any blood pressure medication at all. I now weigh around 136 pounds, my blood pressure stays around 105 to 120 over 55 to 65, and my pulse is 53 to 65 beats per minute. God not only saved me from an aneurysm that would have killed most people, but He used it to give me a wake-up call concerning my overall health. I credit my regular exercise as one of the biggest reasons I am still in great shape as I near my eighties. The most important part of my good health, of course, is the infinite grace of God. My only regret is that I wish I had started paying more attention to my health much sooner, but that is often the way it is when you are a younger person. You are healthy most of the time, so you do not think about it until you have a problem. At my age, however, your health is one of the biggest factors when it comes to overall happiness and quality of life, and I am glad the Lord has seen fit to keep me in decent shape.

***

After my aneurysm scare, I bounced right back and got to work. The year 1994 brought with it a slew of new jobs and accomplishments for my company, especially when it came to wiring up buildings. I remember that we did all the electrical work at an industrial plant not that far from where I was living. My plate was full, and my cup was running over because God was wonderfully pouring out His blessings and increasing my business.

In 1998, however, we ran into a problem. There was work coming up at a plant that was being built adjacent to where we were working, and I was under the impression that my company would handle it. All the property—where we were working and the plant next door to us—was owned by the same man, so it threw me for a loop when I found out another contractor would be coming in to take on the work at the new plant. I felt betrayed in a way—like I had been cheated. As soon as that thought crossed my mind, I immediately corrected myself. I am only human, but I had seen how the Lord had worked in my life, and I was still open to receiving His message whenever He was ready to reveal to me what His plan was for my life. He had called me to do something special for Him, but He had yet to show me what it was. It was important for me to strive in every way to be as free as I could humanly get from thoughts like jealousy and greed, so I took it before Him. I needed Him to set me right. Of course, I would have liked to have taken on the work at the new plant, but only if it were His will and only if it were in line with His plan for me. In this way of thinking, it did not take me long to calm myself and remember that none of my success truly came from my own endeavors. He had given me the tools and opportunities, and He had set everything in motion. If I were to get this work, the money would never really be mine, and I should instead use it to bless others and give back to Him through tithing. With this renewed perspective, I prayed about the situation. For good measure, I went a step further and walked next door from where I was working. I walked along the land where the new plant was going to be built, and I thanked God for this new opportunity, whether it would benefit my company or someone else's. Regardless of who got the work, I prayed that it would bring glory to the Lord.

I continued to wait and pray and found out that the other contractor would indeed do the work at the new plant next door. There is no doubt that I was disappointed, but I accepted the outcome, as I told God I would. A year passed, and I had almost forgotten about the whole thing until I got a call informing me that I would, indeed, be given the electrical work at the new plant. Understand that sometimes God does not answer prayers right away, and sometimes He answers them in a way you would never expect. You cannot rush Him. Even though I ended up getting the work, that situation taught me a lot about being grateful to God for everything He gives us and never forgetting about who is really in charge. He humbled me and helped me to step back and see the world in a less self-centered way, and for that, I am truly thankful.

Since the other contractor had already worked on the new plant for a year, I was not sure how much work would be available. My thoughts went back to the tangled mess of wires I had first encountered in the other plant close to home, and I worried that I might be walking into another situation in which I would have to clean up someone else's mess. There again, that job—while tedious and exhausting—had been the catalyst that led me to start my own company. I decided I would take on any work that was available at the new plant and give it my all. Besides, I had never planned to get that work anyway, so any work the new plant provided my company would be a gift. Once the time came, I was relieved and excited to find out that the scope of the work would be truly enormous. No, we would not be the cleanup crew, and we would not have to deal with anyone else's failings. It turned out to be a challenging job, but my employees were up to the task. They made me proud, and together we all scored a huge win for the company. The work on this project lasted from 1999 all the way to 2001. By the time it was done, we had wired up the plant for the production of their products, as well as the utility building that housed seven chillers and air compressors, plus the control room, the warehouse, and a cooling tower.

I thanked God for this work and especially for how it came about. He did not have to give it to me, but He did.

After that job was done, we jumped right on to more work. It seemed like everyone wanted us to do their jobs, and we were ready for it all. From August 2001 until May 2002, we wired another plant and did all the electrical work for several more projects. Work continued through 2005. We sure were a busy bunch, and it did not show any signs of slowing down one bit.

All this time, we were working as hard as we could go, but we were careful not to push ourselves too hard or too fast. I saw all this work as blessings upon blessings, and I made sure not to let those blessings turn sour by allowing them to cause a rift between myself and my family. Whenever possible, I made sure to be available for them. It has always been important for me to never lose sight of why I do what I do because it is not all about the money. A lot of business owners get things backward and allow their businesses to take over their lives and drive a wedge between themselves and their loved ones, but I have taken great pains to guard against that.

In 2005, I received a call from the owner of a chemical plant in Georgia. As it happened, he also owned a small plant in Mississippi that had been damaged during Hurricane Katrina. He asked me to send a crew to repair the damage, and I agreed. Katrina devastated that whole region of the country, and it took a long time to rebuild. The news showed us all the people who had lost their homes and loved ones during that hurricane, so I had some idea of how bad it was down there. Since plenty of people depended on that plant for their livelihoods, this was an especially important job for my company. I knew that many of them had lost so much from the storm, and some of them were living with family members or renting out hotel rooms, clinging to their jobs at that plant to see them through it all. I thought back to how I felt when our house burned, and I'd had to travel all the way to Alaska just to make ends meet. If we could help get that plant back up and running, it would go a long way toward getting that entire community back on its feet.

Since there were no hotels or motels available for many miles, my employees pulled travel trailers down there, so they would have a place to stay. The damage was more extensive than we had previously thought, but my employees are some of the best around, and they dove right into the work. They ended up staying there from September 2005 to January 2006, and when it was done, I made sure to leave a small crew there to do maintenance and minor repairs. I still had people there up until 2017, just to make sure everything was in tip-top shape. Today, the community around that plant has rebounded and gone back to normal. I am glad that my company had the chance to play a part in that. It really is a joy to give back in any way you can.

After the work was done at the plant in Mississippi, we set our sights on jobs closer to home once again. From 2006 to 2008, most of the work was in or close to where I was living and the plant down in Florida. Once 2008 rolled around, it brought with it another challenge, and this time it hit close to home.

By this time, Deloris had been putting off a particular surgery for about a year. The surgery was not in relation to anything life-threatening, so there really was not any rush to get it done, and I made sure not to push her into doing something she did not want to do yet.

Now, Deloris' mother lived in Waycross during that time, and her sister Gwen lived up in Atlanta. Unbeknownst to her, her mother and sister had a phone conversation, as they did from time to time, and they decided to pray together. During their prayers, the Holy Spirit began to speak to both of their spirits about Deloris' health. They knew she had been putting off her surgery for a while, but the Holy Spirit made it clear that something was wrong and that the surgery needed to take place immediately. According to their interpretation, it was ordered by the Lord for her to get the surgery. They called her as soon as they could and let her know how serious it was and how plainly the Holy Spirit had given them this message. As much as Deloris did not want to rush into surgery, she took heed and set up an appointment with her doctor as soon as she could.

The doctor was confused. There did not seem to be anything wrong with her. Still, he saw the seriousness on her face and went ahead with the usual tests and blood work.

She urged him to do the surgery as soon as possible, but he replied that it would take some time to set it all up. She told him that she understood and set up the surgery for the soonest opening they had.

When the time came, I drove her to the hospital and waited while they took her back to get ready for surgery. She had told me about the message her mother and sister had delivered earlier, and I was there to support her in her decision. Receiving a message from the Lord is not something to take lightly. I had learned that after receiving my own messages from Him, and after seeing the wonderful blessings He had already bestowed upon us. Though I did not understand it, I knew it was His will and that it should be done just as He had commanded.

Neither of us knew what to expect as we entered the hospital. I waited for her after they took her away to be prepared for surgery. My thoughts raced from one thing to another. Why did she need the surgery now? Was something wrong? What was God preparing for our lives? I did not know what to think, but I tried to calm myself and remember that everything was in His hands. Whatever happened would be well with my soul.

A waiting room can be a lonely place, especially when you are in that state of mind. It does not help that you are surrounded by people just like you, waiting to get some of the best or some of the worst news of their lives. It occurred to me that God was at work in the lives of all those people. Some of them were there for minor ailments, but I am sure some of them were just an hour or two away from having their hearts broken, and it struck me that we are all so fragile. A person's life can get derailed out of nowhere, and oftentimes it is never the same afterward.

I skimmed through every magazine they had in that waiting room at least five times. Each time a doctor or nurse walked by, I popped my head up, thinking they were coming to tell me something about Deloris. It was a good thing I had given up smoking long before that because I would have been chain-smoking in the parking lot the whole time. After about three hours, the doctor came out to meet me. When I stood to greet him, I saw the look on his face. He had probably delivered this news plenty of times during his career, but I guess you never really get used to turning someone's life upside down.

I knew something important was going to happen that day. God does not command you to have surgery for no reason. Still, I thought it would be good news, or at least nothing horrible. When he told me they had found cancer during the surgery, it took me a second before the reality of the situation hit me. *Surely they've made a mistake*, I thought. *She's been as fit as ever lately. That doesn't make sense.* As the seriousness of his words hit home, I felt a crushing sense of despair. Anxiety, fear, frustration, rage—all these emotions descended on me like a pack of wolves. I thought back to the girl I had met when we were just teenagers and how we had grown together. We had been through tremendous difficulties, and she was always right there by my side through it all as the true Christian woman that God had blessed me with. Suddenly it hit me that we might not have much time left together, and the thought made me weak in the knees. I could not lose her like this. While those thoughts swirled in my mind, I realized it was all out of my hands. My wife was lying on a gurney somewhere with a disease that kills people every day, and there was not a thing I could do about it. I wanted to be with her, to help her, to make her all better, but I could not. The doctor continued by saying the remainder of the surgery would take around six hours. He said some other things, but at that point, I was too upset to really hear him.

Once he had left to go back to Deloris' surgery, I left the building in a huff and made a beeline for my truck in the parking lot. I have never been one to get emotional, but I will admit there are times when it is perfectly acceptable for a grown man to cry. I had cried over my mother and grandmother when they were taken from me, and I feel no shame in telling you that I wept like a child right there in my truck that day. My heart was heavy, to say the least, and I did the only thing I knew that would give me any kind of relief—I talked to the Father. Sobbing, wiping my eyes, I prayed to Him right out loud and asked Him for His guidance to help me through this. I asked Him to heal my sweet, wonderful, irreplaceable wife. This went on for a while, but suddenly I felt a strange calmness wash over me. While I was in the midst of some of the worst emotional anguish I had ever felt, He spoke to my heart, asking me whose report did I believe? It all made perfect sense. I told Him, "I believe Your report." Without understanding exactly how it would happen, I knew then that God would save her. I realized that what had just happened had occurred many times before in my life. The devil was continuing his relentless pursuit to destroy my family and tear down what God had blessed me with. He had not been able to get to me yet, so it made sense that he would try and go after Deloris since he knew that taking her from me would just about destroy me completely. That is how the devil works. If you are doing anything in the service of God the Father, he will not be able to stand it for very long. He will come after you, and if he cannot get to you, he will go after those closest to you. You may not believe this, but I am here to tell you that the devil is real, and he will not stop until he gets what he wants. He wants you to fail, and he wants you to hurt. He wants you to turn your back on God, and he will work on your mind and your heart, or the minds and hearts of your friends and family, until he succeeds. In my case, Deloris and I were already too faithful and committed to our walk with God. Satan would have had a tough time attacking either of us spiritually, so he decided to attack her physically. It is important for you to understand that I do not believe every cancer diagnosis means you are not right with God or that the devil is trying to kill you. Please do not misunderstand what I am saying. In this case, cancer was simply the tool that the devil chose to use against us.

    I left my truck with a completely different frame of mind. The hospital waiting room did not have the same claustrophobic, dreary feel to it compared to when I had left there just a little while before. It would still be several hours before the doctor would return, but I reminded myself of 2 Timothy 1:7 (KJV), "For God hath not given us the spirit of fear; but of power, and of love, and of a sound mind." I believed God's report concerning my wife, and I was persuaded that He is "able to do exceeding abundantly above all that we ask or think, according to the power that worketh in us," just as it says in Ephesians 3:20 (KJV). Whenever we ask according to His will, He will help us. Glory to God in the highest for that!

It was with the comfort of those scriptures and others that I sat, patiently waiting for the outcome of what was happening not far away in the hospital. Eventually, they called me back to Deloris' room, where I met yet another doctor. This gentleman introduced himself and explained that he was a cancer specialist. I was not sure what to expect, but he was smiling and seemed excited to meet me. He started off by saying that he wished he could tell everyone what had happened because it was not every day that something like this took place. I had been optimistic ever since God had spoken to my heart out in my truck, but now I simply smiled and nodded as he began telling me about the surgery. Whatever had happened, something told me that everything was going to be all right.

He started right in with the best news of all—they had gotten all the cancer. He said it was difficult because there was a paper-thin piece of skin between the cancer cells and Deloris' lymph nodes. Normally, there would have been a low chance of success in this situation based on how close the cancer was to her lymph nodes already. It was especially difficult because there was no way to get in there with a scalpel and remove the cancer. Thankfully, the hospital had a medical-grade laser, and he used it to cut the cancer out of her. To hear him tell it, the cancer cells just burned right away with no problem. In his estimation, the rate of the cancer's growth meant it would have eaten through that thin layer of skin not in a matter of months or weeks but in just a few hours. If we had waited much longer, we would have been having a much, much more serious conversation.

Praise be to the Holy Father for His infinite mercy and love! I am thankful that my wife has always been an ideal woman of God and that her family also walks with the Lord. Had things been different, or if she had been a different kind of person, surrounded by quite different people, the Father may not have seen fit to send her that lifesaving message just when she needed to hear it the most. I maintain that her surgery was, in fact, ordered by God, and out of that near tragedy, He once again showed us how powerful, how caring, and how loving He truly is. You may have noticed a pattern in this book, and if so, that is because it has been the thread that has been woven throughout my entire life. Every time things look grim, when there is no way forward, and every outcome is bleak, God intervenes. He worked wonderous miracles in the Bible, and He has done the same for my family and me. He is not finished working on this earth. Never forget that Satan is still quite busy himself, but nothing he does can last for long in the face of the Almighty, the one who is, has, and will forever be in charge. I want you to think about this whenever you are laid low by something bad in your life and cling to the Father for dear life. If you are not a believer, you might find some of this very unusual, or you might chalk it up to mere coincidences, and that is okay. I cannot make you believe in Him if you do not already, but I would like for you to at least consider that He is real. When you open your mind to that possibility, you might begin to see His works in your life. I have no doubt about all He has done for my family and me, and I hope my life might help you to come just a little bit closer to accepting Him into your own life.

The doctor finished by saying that Deloris would feel quite sick for a while after her surgery and that she should expect pain and bleeding for a time. Honestly, I did not mind that at all. I would gladly do whatever it took to care for her and see to it that she was back to her normal self. All that mattered was she was still here with me, and she was not going anywhere.

The doctor shook my hand and wished us well, then left me his number in case we needed him or had any questions. I am still thankful for him. Whether he knew it or not, he was an instrument and a witness to a bona fide miracle that day. I sat beside Deloris' bed while she rested. I had been so wired that whole time that I had not even realized how tired I was, but when I settled into the little chair beside her bed, I could not sleep. Instead, I watched Deloris as she rested peacefully just a few feet away from me. I imagine she had been under anesthesia the entire time and had no idea what had happened. I was glad she had not seen me the way I had been just a few hours before. I was a lost, broken man on the cusp of losing her forever—or so I thought. Now, here I was, safe and secure in the comfort of knowing that God had brought us out of the pit of despair yet again. He saved her for me. I have plenty of things to be grateful to Him for. That is one of the purposes of this book. Saving Deloris from her cancer is high on my list, though. I have said it before, and I will say it again because it bears repeating—I do not know where I would be without her in my life.

When Deloris awoke, I was right there by her side. I told her to take it easy. My wife has many good qualities, but one of them is stubbornness. She said she was not hurting at all. In fact, she tried to get up from her bed. Of course, I tried to keep her in bed for fear that she might hurt herself. She said she was not hurting or bleeding and seemed intent on getting up and moving around, just like she had before the surgery. Still hooked up to IVs and all sorts of equipment, she just sat up, threw her legs over the side of the bed, grabbed onto the stainless-steel stand that held her IV bag, and started to pick up and go just like she always had. It took some strong convincing, but I managed to get her back into her bed, at least for a while. I know I have talked about how nurturing, caring, and supportive she can be, but she really can be headstrong when she needs to be. She is tough, and she does not let anything slow her down for long. In that way, we are a lot alike, and I am glad about that. She means everything to me, and I have done all I can over the years to do the same for her.

Although she did not like the idea, she got plenty of rest at the hospital. Once visiting hours were over, I would have to leave. This was hard on me, to say the least, but with the doctors and nurses there and the Great Physician watching over her, I knew she was well cared for. Other family members came to visit her, of course, but when her sister came to visit, it was certainly a special occasion. You see, it was a four-hour trip for her sister to make it there. She arrived at around two o'clock in the morning, and she was so excited to see Deloris that she did not realize the hospital had been locked up for the night by the time she arrived. Deloris' sister simply parked in the visitor's lot, then strolled right up to the main doors. These were automated double doors, of course, as most hospitals have. When they did not slide open for her to enter, she placed one hand on the doors and prayed. Almost immediately, the doors opened, and she walked right in. She had not made it far down the hallway when a guard stopped her. "How did you get in?" he asked. In a matter-of-fact way, she told him what had happened, but he did not believe her.

"Ma'am," he said, "I locked those doors myself just a few hours ago."

Deloris' sister merely gestured toward the doors and watched with some amusement as the guard struggled to understand what had happened. The Lord had allowed her into the hospital to see her sister. Since she was already inside and the guard could not find any signs of forced entry, he had no choice but to let her stay.

Deloris was back home within three days, and I did my best to care for her. I was amazed at how well she was doing, but I did not want her to overexert herself since sometimes your mind says you are all better when your body is not quite there. I kept watching for signs of problems, but there were, thankfully, very few of those. Within three weeks, she was out in the yard raking leaves as though nothing had happened. I thank God for that. Not only had He reached down and saved her just in time, but He stayed right there with her throughout her recovery. Whenever we have needed Him the most, He has been right there with us.

Chapter 7

Now this story jumps forward to the year 2010.

Ever since God spoke to me back in 1977, His purpose for my life was never far from my mind. He healed me physically in 1980; then, He healed me financially starting in 1990. He had done exactly as He had promised, but I was still on the lookout for any sign of what kind of work I would do for Him. Well, it would not be long before He revealed His plan to me.

In the meantime, I waited, watched, and prayed. My company continued to grow, and those little paychecks that had first started to come in from my company in the mid-1990s had grown quite a lot. My company was going strong until we hit a little snag. There was some important work coming up down in Plaquemine, Louisiana, and it was likely I would be the contractor to get it. Nothing had been promised, but it all seemed like a done deal at the time. When it came down to it, though, they ended up bringing in another contractor. To say I was disappointed would be an understatement, but I had learned a valuable lesson back when I had lost out on that big job before, and I remembered how I had handled it back then. By this time, money was not much of a problem for my family and me. This is not to brag but to explain to you the role money eventually played in my life. Since we were no longer struggling financially, I had shifted my entire mindset about money. Now it truly was something I could use to bless others since it had all come to me by way of the Father's blessings, anyhow. My disappointment in losing out on the Louisiana job was not due to a loss of income for myself, but I knew it would feed the families of my employees. To me, my employees are as close to family as you can get without being related by blood. I make sure to hire only the best people I can find. They take care of me by giving it their all on the job sites, and I take care of them as best I can because they are important to me. Beyond that, I had, by this time, begun regularly donating to local churches, organizations, and individuals in need. A lot of the time, these blessings were done anonymously because I do not want them to be about me—I want them to be about the Lord.

That is why I wanted the Louisiana job to come through. I did not want it to happen for me, but for all those people I could help. While I waited for God to show me what He wanted me to do in His service, I decided I could not go wrong by giving back what I had been given.

It was for these unselfish reasons that Deloris and I decided to go to the job site down in Louisiana, even though I had not been given the job. We had something else in mind entirely. You get to see some pretty country when you drive from Georgia down to Louisiana. It had been a long time since I had to travel that far for work, but this did not feel like work at all.

We arrived at the job site and toured the grounds and as much of the surrounding land that was open to the public, all the while holding hands and silently praying. Once we were alone out there on the grounds, we prayed together that God might see fit to open a door of opportunity for my company so that we could, in turn, bless others with the majority of the earnings. I am thankful God has put me in a position to do as Psalm 37:4 (KJV) instructs, "Delight thyself also in the Lord; and he shall give thee the desires of thine heart." When you do your utmost to align the desires of your heart with the desires of God, you reach a new level of happiness and fulfillment.

After we had gone to the job site and prayed over the land, I was content with knowing we had done our part. God knew what was in my heart, and He knew I would make good on what I wanted to do with the earnings from the job. That was enough for me. I did not know when He would answer those prayers, but I fully trusted Him, and I would be happy with whatever decision He made.

A year later, it happened. A call came in inviting me to go down to Louisiana to meet with the owner of the company I was working for at the time. This was also the gentleman who owned the land at the chemical plant near where I had worked previously, so I knew He was aware of everything I had accomplished. Well, let us say he was aware of everything that God had helped me accomplish.

During our meeting, he told me I would indeed be awarded work in Louisiana, except I would be working at a brand-new plant, in charge of installing all the new electrical systems. This came with a catch, however; he intended to track my progress meticulously, then decide whether or not the job was successful and up to his own standards.

Like I said earlier, I only hire the best people, and I only surround myself with the most capable people I can find. A lot was riding on this job. If we succeeded, he would surely award us with more work. I knew my people could handle it, as we were always up for any challenge that came our way. I made the trip down to Louisiana, but this time it was with the sweet satisfaction that God had once again answered my humble prayers. I was excited to see what He would do for my company and me, and I was looking forward to giving back to the people in my life, as well as my local community.

It turned out to be tough work, but my people handled it with ease. It did not take long before the owner met with me personally. He not only had wonderful things to say about the work we were doing but also that we were saving him money at the same time. We had made him quite a happy man, it seemed. In return, he informed me that my company would be given all the work previously given to three other companies. Talk about a blessing and a new challenge! At first, it was overwhelming. One company rarely has the opportunity or the resources to handle that much work, but we dug in and got to it, as always. By the time 2012 rolled around, we were knee-deep in work down in Louisiana. I stayed on for six months straight before heading back to Georgia, but before I left, I received the answer from God that I had been looking for ever since that fateful day in 1977.

I had rented a small apartment not far from the job site, which was customary when working long jobs like that one. It was a normal day, and I decided to relax for a while after work and watch a little bit of television. I cannot remember what program I was watching at the time, but for some reason, one of the commercials caught my attention. The commercial was presented by a rabbi who represented the International Fellowship of Christians and Jews. Now, I had always considered myself a friend of the Jews and saw them as God's people. I knew they had been oppressed ever since biblical times, and the memories of the holocaust were still not that far away since I had grown up hearing about it all. It broke my heart to think that God's chosen people had suffered so much indignity and injustice even in modern times and that many of them still struggled even in the twenty-first century. This rabbi was talking about the need to bring all the Jews of the world home to Israel, or at least the ones who wanted to return to their homeland. What really struck me was when he said that he was trying to bring them back on "wings of eagles," just as it says in the Scripture. I felt an instant connection to this man, a sort of kinship that I could not quite explain, and I instantly respected him and what he was trying to do.

I was sitting on a small sofa, and there was a walkway behind me. Suddenly, I heard a voice say, "Bring My people home." I turned around but found no one else in the room. It occurred to me then that I had locked the door when I had gotten home, as well, and there was no way anyone could have gotten in.

Now, I know what you are thinking, even if you are already a believer. "Tim was hallucinating," you say. "He's making this up," is what you might be thinking.

Friends, I promised you at the very beginning of this book that I would tell you the truth. I also told you that some of those truths might be difficult for you to believe, but rest assured, this is what happened. I am telling it to you exactly as it occurred that day in 2012.

I want to take a moment to talk about the reality of how God speaks to us. You may not have experienced it, but He communicates with us all the time. In my case, it was direct and unmistakable. Regardless, this is a very real thing. Think about that for a moment. How else would we know if we are saved unless He speaks to us through His inspired Scripture? Today, it is still true that "the Spirit itself beareth witness with our spirit, that we are the children of God," just as it says in Romans 8:16 (KJV). Serious communication takes place when God speaks to our spirit and guides us to do His perfect will for our lives. The hardest part about all this is being sensitive enough to that guidance. If we are not sensitive to what He says through His Word and by His Spirit, then He sometimes chooses to speak to us by whatever means are available. Remember in the Old Testament when He spoke to Balaam through the mouth of a donkey? That is what I am talking about. The reason He was so direct with me might be because I am hard-headed at times, and I needed something clear so I would know it was Him.

Whether or not you are willing to do His will, God is sovereign. He can speak to your heart. Because He worked with me for so long to make me into what He wanted me to be, I was, by that time, completely happy to do His will and help bring peace to those He loves. That is why I had no reservations about helping to bring His people home.

Regardless of whether you believe it or not, I'm living proof that God really does communicate to His redeemed children through His Holy Spirit. That is what happened on that day, and it opened my eyes to what He wanted me to do—bring His people home. Some go into the ministry and preach. Others devote their time to going on mission trips and even move to far-flung parts of the world to help those in need by installing electricity and running water. We all have gifts and abilities to serve Him and His work. He made us all unique, and we all have a place on this team of His. For my part, He chose for me to bless His own people through the fruits of my labor, which have all been given to me by Him. Ever since that day, I have made it an utmost priority to give all I can to the International Fellowship of Christians and Jews. To my mind, it is important that Christians stand with the Jews in spite of the antagonistic spirit that stands against both Jews and Christians. I believe that nothing can prevent us from successfully accomplishing His divine will because of the promise of Romans 8:31 (KJV), which states, "If God be for us, who can be against us?" Also, if we will be for God, who can stand against us? In all I do, I strive to be on His side and to do His will. His chosen people are important to Him, which means they are important to me.

I have learned a great deal about the Jews and their culture since being led to do this work. Returning to or even visiting the homeland is a special thing for God's people. There is even a word just for that: "aliyah," which means "ascent." For so long, the Jewish people have been dispersed across this old world without a home of their own until 1948, when the State of Israel was established. It is so enjoyable for me to give to that organization because it does not just help them to travel to the homeland. Besides getting them there, the donations help to feed and clothe them. Many of them suffered in dire poverty without even basic living necessities that many people take for granted. Over time, I carried on some correspondence with the rabbi I'd seen that day on television, as well as his daughter.

Sadly, the rabbi passed away in 2019, but his daughter has since taken his place. She has done an excellent job. I am honored to be a part of such a worthy cause, and it does my heart so much good to know that I am helping to change lives for the better.

***

It was wonderful to be back home after being gone for six months in Louisiana. God had finally revealed His plan to me, and I set about doing His will. Can you guess what was about to happen? That is right, Satan was already building a plan against me, and he would soon put that plan in motion. He had attacked me physically with kidney stones, and then he had attacked Deloris with cancer. God, however, intervened and showed the devil that we belonged to the Almighty. Now the devil would try again, except this time he would come after me more directly and with much more anger and violence than ever before.

It all started out as a typical Thursday in 2013. I woke up at 3:30 a.m. A lot of people might think that it is way too early to be getting out of bed, but it works for me. It gives me time to shave, shower, and greet the day. Today, I visit my prayer closet each morning to spend time with the Father, but back in 2013, I was still communing with Him during my drive to work. I went about my usual morning routine, but as it came time to leave, everything changed. I felt an unnatural sense of urgency for some reason. It was as though some unseen force had grabbed me by the hand and kept ushering me to my truck. Since it was payday, it was my responsibility to take all the checks and some cash to work to pay my employees. I shrugged and figured it was just my mind wanting to get there as soon as I could, so I could pay my employees what they had earned that week.

By this point in my life, my company was headquartered about forty-five minutes from where I had grown up. This was where we were keeping our offices since we had moved out of that humble travel trailer years before. It did not take me long to get there, and I had traveled that route many, many times by that point. I often thought I could have safely gotten there and back blindfolded if I had to.

It was still early in the morning, and the roads around my home are usually empty except for a few stray cars passing through or maybe a log truck or tractor-trailer. The sun was not all the way up yet when I left my house, but I could faintly see the dew on the grass on the shoulder of the road. I eased along until I had made it to a long straightaway, then I pushed my truck a little. I need to admit to you here that I have always liked to drive fast. It is because I like to feel like I am headed somewhere instead of just puttering along. This is something that the Lord is still working on with me. Once I had gotten my speed up to about sixty-five miles per hour, I set the cruise control and started in with my morning prayers, thanking God for what He had done for me over the years, as well as asking Him for His guidance in whatever the day might bring. I remember changing lanes, and it was not long before I found myself behind a loaded dump truck. In the half-darkness of the early morning, I thought the dump truck was barreling along ahead of me. By the time I realized what was happening, it was already too late. Instead of cruising along ahead of me in the same lane, he had stopped on the road. This would have worked out fine for both of us if it had not been for one crucial thing: his brake lights were out.

By the time I realized what was happening, there was no time for me to even hit the brakes. The last thing that ran through my mind before I hit him was, *Out of all the days to get in a wreck; it would have to be payday.*

***

I woke up, but I could not move. I was surrounded by what looked like the inside of my truck cab, but everything seemed out of place. For just a second, I thought I was dead. After blinking a few times, I turned my head just a little and tried to focus. The windshield of my truck looked like a massive spider web from where the safety glass had cracked. The impact had sent all the checks and cash flying, and they littered the cab of my truck. My poor steering wheel was missing a chunk about the size of my head, and what was left of the airbag trailed down out of the middle of the steering wheel. Something warm ran down into my right eye, and I knew it was blood.

I do not know how long I had been unconscious, but it seemed like the ambulance was there in just a minute or two, lights flashing, sirens wailing. Through the cracked windshield and the smashed driver door, I picked out four shapes walking toward me from the ambulance. Even in my addled state, I realized these were the EMTs, but I thought it was strange that they were not walking any faster. I tried to sit up and wave at them, but I still could not move much at all. I wanted to say something, but it was as if my entire body was pinned down against the driver's seat. I looked down at my lap, but I did not see anything holding me down. My legs, from what I could tell, were free, as well as my arms.

I could not see too well out the driver's side window, and the lights from the ambulance lit up the cracked windshield until it all looked like a kaleidoscope. A female EMT peered in at me through the windshield, then eased around and looked at me through the driver's side window. I remember her turning and saying, "He's dead. Get the body bag." She did not yell it, and it dawned on me that she was talking to someone behind her whom I could not see because of the cracked windshield and the A-pillar of my truck. I tried to move and let her know I was okay, but I was still paralyzed for some reason. They turned off the sirens then, and I saw her walk to the dump truck. For the first time, I gauged where it was in relation to my own truck, and I knew something was off. There was plenty of space between my truck and the back of the dump truck, which did not make any sense. I do not know if you know anything about dump trucks, but they are not little bitty things. They weigh a great deal, especially when they are loaded down with dirt.

The female EMT walked past the front of my truck, and the driver of the dump truck met her. I could barely make out what they were saying, but I overheard the dump truck driver tell her, "There's no way he lived through that. I have never seen a pickup hit something that hard. He pushed my truck ten, maybe even twelve feet."

Before long, more people had congregated where the female EMT and the dump truck driver stood. After some debate, they agreed that it would normally take a bulldozer to push a loaded dump truck that far.

From what I could tell, they had all written me off as dead. I felt powerless. I wanted to get out and show them I was okay, but for some reason, I still could not move. The thought occurred to me then that I might have broken my neck or my back, and a wave of nausea rushed over my body. I pictured myself confined to a wheelchair, unable to live the active, abundant life I had worked so hard for and had been so blessed to finally have.

While I pondered the reason for my immobility, the female EMT broke away from the group and stood beside my truck, peering in at me as best as she could through the cracked glass.

She must have been holding out some sliver of hope for me because she whispered, "Baby, are you okay?"

"Baby," I stammered, "don't put me in that body bag."

Without hesitation, she spun around, waved her arms, and shouted, "Come help me! He is alive! Bring the stretcher, quick!" The rest of the team rushed to my truck, but they could not get the driver's side door to open. The impact must have warped my truck's frame and pinned the door shut, so one of the EMTs ran back to the ambulance. He came back with what looked like a pickaxe. The front of my truck looked like a crushed soda can, and he took great care as he climbed up onto what used to be the hood of my truck.

He swung the pickaxe several times, but my windshield did not budge. The head of the pickaxe bounced back with each strike, and he finally leaned back, looked at the female EMT who had discovered I was still alive, then shook his head.

"That doesn't make any sense," she said. "It acts like he has bulletproof glass."

Looking back, that was funny. I know some characters in action movies and real-world celebrities and dignitaries often have bulletproof glass installed in their vehicles, but to think that I did was odd. I was just me. At the time, it was no laughing matter. Later, I learned that the safety glass in windshields normally breaks apart in one piece to help people be rescued and to keep the glass from shattering and cutting the occupants in case of an accident, so it made sense that she was puzzled.

As it happened, my grandson chose to use the same road on his way to work. He must have recognized my truck because he ran to the passenger's side door before anyone could stop him. With no trouble at all, he opened the door. I turned my head just enough to look him in the eye as he opened the door, and I saw tears streaming down his cheeks. "Over here!" he pleaded. "Come get him out of there!"

Carefully, they took me out of my truck, laid me out on the stretcher, then loaded me up into the back of the ambulance. They cleaned me up as best they could and wiped the blood off my forehead. Little by little, I regained the full use of my voice and my arms and legs. When the ambulance stopped, they brought me out, and I saw that we were in an open field. I heard the unmistakable whirring of helicopter blades coming from somewhere over the tree line. Now, I had been on all sorts of planes and ships, but I had never flown in a helicopter before. If only this had been under better circumstances, I might have enjoyed it.

We were in the air for all of the twenty-eight minutes before touching down at the nearest major hospital in the region, which was in Savannah, Georgia. I have never been one to get sick much, so I had not spent much time in hospitals other than when Deloris was having her surgery. Well, I was about to make up for the lost time. They wasted no time in getting me to the trauma unit, and before I could blink, six doctors and two nurses came rushing into the room, getting me ready for what I assumed would be an emergency surgery. I had no idea what kind of injuries I had sustained, but I remember thinking that I did not hurt all that bad for a man who'd just lived through what I'd lived through. For five and a half hours, those doctors and nurses ran every kind of test imaginable, poking and prodding me like I was a science experiment. I waited for them to put me under so they could cut on me or do whatever it was they needed to do, but they never used any anesthesia. There was no surgery.

Once all of that was done, the physician-in-charge came to my bedside. There had been no time to explain much to me, so I had no idea what kind of news he was bringing me.

***

Sometimes your mind can be your worst enemy.

I had not been given much of a chance to move around by that point, so my mind wandered. Would I have permanent problems from the wreck? Was there some internal damage that I did not know about? I assumed that the doctors had put me on any number of pain medications to help me through the trauma, so I had no way to tell how bad off I was. No one had given me the slightest information regarding the outcome of all the tests they had run on me, but when you hear about a seventy-one-year-old getting into a head-on collision, the results are usually not good. I was glad to be alive, but what if I was paralyzed in some way? How would I provide for my family?

All these thoughts swirled through my mind as the physician in charge stood beside my bed, waiting to deliver the news. Now, I know that doctors usually are not supposed to let you know how they feel when they deliver results to you. They will show you they are sympathetic when they give you sad news, or they share in your joy when they give you good news. It is part of their job to be as objective as possible. This physician in charge, however, had a slight look of disbelief on his face, and I could not tell whether this was a good thing or a dreadful thing.

Finally, after what seemed like quite a long time, he spoke.

He told me that the tests had taken five and a half hours for a particularly good reason—they were looking for signs of internal bleeding, broken bones, or damaged organs. They had taken extra time checking out my head, he told me, since I had hit the steering wheel with such force that a chunk of the wheel was missing. The impact had caused a gash and lots of swelling, but he went on to say that all the swelling was external. Considering the speed at which I was traveling, what I had hit, and how I had hit it, this was completely out of the ordinary. According to him, he said the wreck should have killed me.

As soon as he said all of this, I only smiled because I knew that God had once again stepped in and said, "No!" He had shown me that He was still very much in control and that I had more work to do for Him. Since they could not find anything wrong with me other than the cut on my head and the swelling—neither of which were life-threatening—the physician in charge had no choice but to discharge me. In his own words, he said, "I can't even find a broken toe on you. I'm going to release you."

There I was, worried that I would have debilitating problems for the rest of my life due to the wreck, but they could not even find a broken toe. To be honest, my head did hurt some, but other than that, it is amazing to think that I walked away from that wreck with only a cut and some swelling. God really does protect us from the snares and attacks of Satan. I knew then that everything was going to be okay.

I want to take a moment now to give thanks to God for what He did for me that day. His mercy and grace endure forever. I rejoice because I know my help comes from the Father, just as it says in Psalm 121:1–3 (KJV). I completely agree with the psalmist of that verse, who wrote,

> I will lift up mine eyes unto the hills, from whence cometh my help. My help cometh from the Lord, which made heaven and earth. He will not suffer thy foot to be moved: he that keepeth thee will not slumber.

Friends, God sure does not take a break when it comes to looking out for us. He has never failed me in any way.

Considering all this, I was understandably thankful, overjoyed, and in awe of the blessings of my Lord. But what came next was the icing on the cake.

Remember when my wife's sister called me in 1977 and delivered the message that I was to do God's will? She is a special woman, and God saw fit to speak through her once again. Before I was released from the hospital, Deloris told me what had happened. She and her sister had been praying for me as soon as they found out about my wreck. Deloris headed to the hospital in Savannah straight away, and her sister left Atlanta as soon as possible. While they were traveling, the Spirit of God began to speak peace into their souls. Both my wife and her sister are sensitive to the movement of God in their lives and in their spirits, and it is a blessing to have such extraordinary people in my life. Not long into her journey to Savannah, my sister-in-law began to speak in tongues. As the Spirit gave utterance, this was the interpretation: "I was with him before the wreck, and I am with him now." Even before I received the good news and discovered there was nothing seriously wrong with me from the wreck, God saw fit to comfort both my wife and sister-in-law with this message. Knowing that the Father was with me gave them tremendous hope in the face of despair. It occurred to me then that God had saved Deloris for me in 2008, and now, in 2013, He had saved me—once again—for her!

I am thankful for this and for the fact that God loves us so much that He has made it possible to communicate directly in this way with His children. You may be wondering why I believe in this so strongly. The answer is simple. First Corinthians 14:13 (KJV) tells us, "Wherefore let him that speaketh in an unknown tongue pray that he may interpret it." I would like to mention another important part of this, and that is the importance of true women of God in a person's life. Women can be used mightily by God. If it is part of His plan, gender does not matter to Him. Just look at the Bible. It is filled with examples of godly women. Joel 2:28–29 (KJV) says,

> And it shall come to pass afterward, that I will pour out my spirit upon all flesh; and your sons and your daughters shall prophesy, your old men shall dream dreams, your young men shall see visions: And also upon the ser-

vants and upon the handmaids in those days will I pour out my spirit.

We are living in those days.

My sister-in-law told Deloris the message God had given her. Up until then, Deloris was driving as fast as she could, terrified of what she might find when she arrived at the hospital. But as soon as she heard this, she slowed down. Her sister returned to Atlanta, confident in the knowledge that I would be okay. This was all due to God's special outpouring of His Spirit, and it was such a special blessing.

In the wake of this latest miracle, Deloris and I were elated. I had not eaten in quite a while, and Deloris had been too upset to even think about a meal, so we decided to stop and get gas, then drop by a restaurant on the way out of Savannah. Now, you might think that after this miracle, we would need to wait a little while before God spoke to either of us again so directly. All the time before, it had been this way. But never underestimate the Spirit of God, my friends. He is always working, and He is always ready to touch your heart and give you the message you need to hear at just the right time you need to hear it.

On the way inside the restaurant, Deloris noticed a man sitting outside on the curb, eating. From the look of him, he was homeless, or at the very least, to have fallen on tough times. For some reason, Deloris felt compelled to talk to this man. To my surprise, she approached him as though they had been friends for years. She struck up a conversation with this man and began telling him all about my wreck and the ways in which God had helped me through it all. Once she was done relaying the story, he told us that he wanted to pray for me and asked if I would, in turn, pray for him. By this time, he had finished his meal, and we invited him to take a few steps back to our vehicle so we could all pray together without the hustle and bustle of people entering and leaving the restaurant. We all gathered at Deloris' vehicle, and the man asked if I was okay and how I was feeling. This would not have stuck out to me, but he said it with such genuine honesty that it surprised me. Now, you may think that this was nothing more than a homeless man or a man who was having a challenging time. You might even think he was simply trying to fleece us for money by faking interest in our lives. You might think that, and you're welcome to do so, but you were not there. There was something special about this gentleman. I assured him that I was fine, and we began to pray. It was not long before he began to speak in tongues. This was even more unexpected because Deloris had not mentioned anything about this particular way that God chooses to communicate with His children. The Holy Spirit gave utterance through this man, and he rendered the interpretation as he was moved upon by the Spirit of God, saying, "I could have raised you from the dead if I had to. I told Satan to take his hands off you. You still have work to do for Me."

All the way home, Deloris and I marveled at the glory of God and how He can use anyone He chooses to deliver His word. How wonderful it is to receive not only the blessings I have received from the Father but to be assured in this way that I was right on course, doing His work, and that He had more in store for me!

***

I am no preacher, although I have learned a lot from some exceptionally good preachers in my time. My story so far—as well as this entire book—is merely my testimony of the wonderful things God can do in a person's life. He has done such amazing things that I cannot help but talk about them. I am so glad I have been redeemed by the blood of Jesus Christ and have the assurance of His word that says in Matthew 26:28 (KJV), "This is my blood of the new testament, which is shed for many for the remission of sins."

All of this can be yours, too. I would like to take just a minute to ask you two simple questions: Do you believe in Jesus? Have you accepted Him as your substitute, the one who took your place at an old rugged cross and paid the ultimate price to wash away your sins and transgressions?

If not, please call upon Him now because He loves you and is not willing that you should perish but come to repentance that you, too, might know the Lord and experience His peace and joy in your soul. John 14:27 (KJV) says, "Peace I leave with you, my peace I give unto you: not as the world giveth, I give unto you. Let not your heart be troubled, neither let it be afraid." Call on Him now because His Word says in Romans 10:13 (KJV) that whoever "shall call upon the name of the Lord shall be saved."

I have been blessed, but beyond that, I have the peace I have just told you about. This is the kind of peace that can only come from the Father, and I would like for you to share in this joy and peace by giving your heart to the Father.

Chapter 8

The wreck happened on a Thursday morning. Although I was released from the hospital and could have returned to work the next day if I had wanted to, I decided to take Friday off, then return to work on Monday.

The supervisors and the men who work for me were in shock. They could not believe that a seventy-one-year-old man showed right back up to work after such an ordeal. I just shrugged and told them I was fine and that it was time for me to get back to work.

For a while after my wreck, everything hummed along without any problems. Things were going so well that the snares of the old devil became just a distant memory. My company continued to grow, thanks to the grace of the Lord, and I wholeheartedly threw myself into my work, as well as donating as much as I could to the International Fellowship of Christians and Jews. Everything seemed right with the world, or so I thought.

Something was brewing, however. Satan had gotten so brave that he had seen fit to physically come against Deloris, then he had come against me. God had saved us both, but what was about to happen was truly despicable. Over the course of the next few years, Satan would come against other members of our family repeatedly.

***

The first person Satan targeted was one of my grandsons while he was on his way to work early one morning in 2013. It was a normal day, and he was going about his business just as he had so many times before, except for one thing. On this day, he decided to pull out his checkbook as he eased up to a stop sign. He was looking over some of his latest transactions one moment, and the next moment he found himself one step away from certain death. As he had been looking at his checkbook, he did not notice that his foot had not fully pressed the brake pedal. He was coming off a side road and onto a major highway, but traffic is usually light around that time of the morning.

Before he realized what was happening, he had rolled up under a semi-truck. It just so happened that the front of his pickup wedged itself under the semi-truck's trailer. Instead of running over my grandson, the semi dragged his truck down the highway for a long way before he could stop. Miraculously, both my grandson and the driver of the semi-truck walked away without a scratch. If that is not a miracle of God, then I do not know what is.

***

A few years later, another one of my grandsons welcomed the birth of his first child. Normally, this would have been a joyous occasion, but there was a serious problem—the child had been born with some of its vital organs on the outside of its body. Naturally, this was a great cause of concern for all of us, especially because children with this problem normally do not live very long. I am happy to report that, as of this writing, their child is doing fine, despite all the odds. Yet again, God has blessed my family.

***

When I tell you the next part of my story, please understand that I will not go too deeply into details, and I am not going to name anyone outright. My purpose is not to slander folks but to show you how God has blessed my family and me. To do this, I must talk about some dreadful things people have done.

These events took place in 2020. To set the scene for the next horrible attack Satan launched against my family, I need to describe the situation that led up to it. One of my relatives, who was in her early twenties at the time, had a boyfriend. She had a son with this boyfriend, but unfortunately, she found herself raising her child alone. She is a sweet girl, and it was not long before she began dating another young man. Everything seemed fine between them, but it became obvious to Deloris and me that something was very wrong with this situation. This new boyfriend started off like the perfect gentleman. He treated her and her child with respect, and it was not long before she became quite close with this young man. As soon as that happened, however, a switch flipped in his mind.

Suddenly, he became obsessed with her. Where he had once been loving, supportive, and thoughtful about giving her space, he now became unnaturally jealous and possessive. He would boast to his friends at work that he had a house and a car, but he was talking about her house and her car. She told us that he acted as though all her possessions were, in fact, his. It is not unusual for a man to treat his girlfriend's child as his own, but she told Deloris and me that this young man went too far, acting as though her child was his property. Little by little, my female relative revealed to us that this young man had a drinking problem. As much as I did not want to meddle in her life, I could not help but think back to my own childhood and my dad's actions. In a strange way, this young man fit the description perfectly. The only redeeming quality was that he hadn't hit her. Now, my female relative had grown up in a less-than-perfect household. While she was concerned about her boyfriend's increasingly disturbing behavior, she may have tolerated it because it seemed normal to her. I am no psychologist, but I have been around long enough to know that sometimes people stay in bad situations or even put themselves into bad situations because of trauma in their pasts. It's easy to say, "Get out of that relationship! You're in danger!" When you are the person living it, however, it is not always that simple. Deloris and I tried to advise her gently, but I have found that if you try to tell someone what to do, they usually dig in their heels and do just the opposite. We both cared deeply for her, but we knew not to push her too hard. It was her life, and it was up to her to make her own decisions. Regardless, I took my concerns to the Father, begging Him not to let things turn violent between them.

Not long after that, the verbal abuse began. I have my suspicions that this had been going on before she admitted it to us, but it was only when things became truly hateful that she told us. This young man used every curse word and belittling phrase he could think up, and it broke my heart to hear her tell us how their relationship was crumbling. Instead of getting out, however, she kept seeing this young man. He was the perfect example of a wolf in sheep's clothing. He started off great, then showed her his dark side. What was really disturbing, though, was how he would manipulate her emotions. Just when she was ready to leave him, he would suddenly switch back to his former self just long enough to draw her back into the relationship. Once they had patched things up, he would unleash the other side of his personality on her once more. I have known of men and women who do this, and while it might not make sense to someone outside of the situation, the other person in the relationship is often caught up in it like a fly in a spider web, emotionally confused and sometimes even spiritually manipulated. I thought back to how my dad had treated my mother, myself, and my siblings, and I knew where this was going, even though I prayed as hard as I could that it would not come to that.

Sure enough, my female relative eventually admitted that her boyfriend had begun to abuse her physically. It was clear that this would not stop and that it would only escalate from there. Still, he continued to play with her mind, giving her just enough of his good side to keep her in the relationship. He would beg her forgiveness, and she would take him back every time. At this point, it was becoming clear to me that this was the work of Satan. He could not attack Deloris or me directly, so he would try and tear down the life of someone remarkably close to us. Once the physical abuse started, I'd had enough. Before that, I did not feel it was my place to meddle in her business. She was an adult, had a good head on her shoulders, and was more than capable of making her own decisions. To hear that her boyfriend was hitting her filled me with rage, and I tried my best to get through to her. She understood what I was trying to tell her, and she agreed with me, but that did not matter. On an emotional level, she was completely hooked on this young man. He was handsome, well-off, charming, charismatic, and well-loved by many people in the community.

Remember when I talked earlier about addiction, and I said addiction could take many forms beyond just drugs, drinking, or smoking? This is a perfect example. My relative, who was a smart person, could not stop seeing this young man because he had set things up so that she would become addicted to him. As far as we knew, he was not abusing her child, but I could tell it was only a matter of time before he crossed that line. Reputation is still an important thing in a small town, and this young man had a great reputation—at least on the surface. It was during this time that my female relative began to really ask around about him, especially when it came to other women he had dated in the past. Strangely enough, she was met with silence and half-answers. It was as though people knew something about him, and they did not want to tell. Small towns can be strange sometimes in that these are places known for never-ending gossip, but they are also good at keeping secrets.

Eventually, she connected with a former girlfriend of this young man. What she learned made my blood boil. According to this former girlfriend, he had started out the relationship just as he had with my female relative—charming, funny, loving, and sincere. It was as though he had spent his entire life learning how to be the perfect gentleman. Over time, however, he plunged her into a pit of despair, using a constant barrage of psychological and emotional warfare until she even doubted her own sanity at times. Thankfully, she had gotten out, but not without a cost. Her physical wounds had healed, but her mind was still in shock from his abuse. It had been a couple of years since she had gotten rid of him, but she still slept with a knife under her pillow just in case he ever broke into her house at night.

At first, my relative did not want to believe this. Friends, this is how the devil can work on a person's mind. Even when she was faced with overwhelming evidence that supported her worst fears, my young relative still had her doubts. Why? People who study the human mind could give you all kinds of reasons. I am sure you have heard of this sort of situation before, and you may even have experienced something like this. It is often difficult to think clearly when you are in love or when you think you are in love. It was clear to me that Satan himself had set this up from the beginning. Those emotions she was feeling were real, but the devil clouded her judgment even further. Helped along by Satan's sinister hand, that young man became her addiction. As we all know, sometimes a person can follow that addiction all the way to the grave. To me, I interpreted the young man's abusive nature as his real self. The nice, loving version of him was just a mask he wore to get her hooked in the beginning.

What happened next was a living nightmare. I am going to tell you what happened on that fateful day, just as it was told to me by my young relative because I was not there myself when it occurred.

One day, the young man picked up my relative and took her to his house. Things had not been going too well between them. By this point, that was normal since the time between his dark behavior and his happy, loving behaviors had begun to last longer and longer. They had an argument, but once things cooled off, she rode with him to a nearby convenience store and picked up some snacks. By this time, it was dark. Instead of going back to the young man's house, however, he took her to a field. They parked and talked some more. All this time, the young man's truck was still running, and its headlights shone across the field. Eventually, she got out of the young man's truck and sat on the ground. The field had been plowed about a year before, and the soil was still soft. My relative waited patiently for the young man to come and join her, but he stayed in the truck. She was not very far away from him, but she could not see what the young man was doing since the headlights were shining in her direction. Instead of getting out of the truck, the young man stepped on the gas pedal. At that moment, the devil had full control of that young man, and he used him as his tool to try and accomplish his evil goal.

At first, she thought he was easing his way toward her, but the truck was moving too fast. When she realized what was happening, it was too late. At the last second, she tried to roll out of the path of the truck, but the front tire caught her. The truck rolled across her back. Instinctively, she turned over, lying now on her back. The young man stopped the truck just after the truck rolled over my relative. In shock, she expected the back tire to roll over her. Instead, the young man threw his truck into reverse. The front tire rolled over her chest, but this time the young man allowed his truck to rest on top of her for just a moment before backing up a few more feet. My relative lay helpless in the field, wracked with pain. The young man sat in his truck for a moment, then he got out of his truck and went to her body. Had God not chosen to place His hand of protection over her, she would have been dead by then, but she had survived. In a flash, the young man scooped her up and threw her in the cab of his truck. Even though she had survived the attack, she could have been paralyzed since she had no way of knowing if her neck was broken. The young man threw her into the passenger side of his truck. Just before he slammed the door shut, he said, "I could've killed you, and no one would've known."

Though her strength was failing her, my relative took out her cell phone and called 911. "Please come and help me," she pleaded with the dispatcher. "He tried to kill me!" The young man sat in the driver's seat, completely unmoved by what he had just done.

"There's nothing wrong with her!" he said, loud enough for the dispatcher to hear. "Don't worry about her!"

They stayed right there in his truck until the ambulance arrived and took my young relative to the hospital. When asked what happened, the young man said it was an accident. According to him, he had no idea my relative was in the path of his truck. He said he thought she had walked off. Keep in mind that this field was many miles away from the young man's house, and my relative had no one she could have gotten to within walking distance of that field.

Naturally, I had no idea this was happening, although I had carried a bad feeling in the pit of my stomach concerning her relationship with this young man. I found out about the attack the next morning, but the authorities were not positive about just what had happened since my relative was too injured to tell them much. Even so, they put two and two together and realized that he had tried to kill her. My mind switched back to the rage I had felt on the day my dad had killed my mother and grandmother, and I wanted to kill that young man. She had done nothing to deserve this, and I wanted to make him pay. I had to fight back my anger and turn my attention toward being there for my relative.

This brings us to yet another miracle in my life. My relative should have been killed that day, but God chose to spare her life. Even so, she did not make it out of that situation without injury. All her ribs had been broken, she was suffering from a collapsed lung, and many of her other bones had been broken under the weight of the truck. According to the police, she would not have survived if the attack had happened on harder ground. The soil in the field gave way just enough to keep her from being completely crushed. She was confined to her hospital bed for a long time, and it is a true miracle of God that she eventually recovered.

What happened next is hard to believe. I lived through it, and I still have a tough time accepting that it happened the way it did.

An investigation followed, and I was sure he would pay for what he had done. This young man had tried to take her life, but he was free to walk the streets, work a job, and live like the rest of us. What made it even worse was the fact that I was powerless. The law had, for whatever reason, not chosen to punish him, so I had no legal right to seek justice for my female relative. This was a truly twisted, perverse situation, but I realized what was going on behind the scenes. Satan had been responsible for this. He had been working in that young man's life for some time, especially when you consider the story of his former girlfriend who was driven to keep a knife under her pillow for protection. My relative was simply his latest victim. She had been targeted by the devil since she was a part of my family, and Satan knew that this attack would hurt me deeply. What was even worse was the fact that this young man was free to find another target. Just as God protects His own, it is true that Satan offers protection to those who do his will. There is no doubt in my mind that the young man who tried to kill my relative was touched by the devil's hand and that he was offered protection. Satan may not be able to stand against God, but you'd better believe that he has his own degree of power in this world, and he will certainly exercise it as much as he can to tear down everything that is of the Lord.

Meanwhile, my relative's struggle was far from over.

During her long, difficult convalescence, she stayed with a family member. This was an older woman who had some issues of her own, and alcohol was one of the biggest of those issues. Although she wanted to help my relative, things turned grim when this older woman began dating a man around her own age. In the beginning, this man was helpful and kind and joined the older woman in caring for my young relative. Before long, everything fell apart. This older man fixated on my relative and would switch between being helpful and being verbally abusive to her. He eventually became obsessed with her, which obviously caused problems between the three of them. As soon as my young relative could get around on her own, she escaped from that situation and never looked back.

I want to take a moment to stress just how important it is to have good people in your life. I have talked about how much of a blessing it is for a man to have a strong woman of God in his life, and I want to say that the same goes for women. To have a boyfriend or a husband who is a man of God is invaluable to a woman because choosing the wrong man can ruin your life. It is just as important to have a support system of family and friends who are upstanding, God-fearing people. I pray for those who do not have that in their lives, and it seems like that has become normal today. Life is difficult enough when you have good people in your corner, but it can be unbearable when you do not have those kinds of people in your life. I would also like to use this part of the story as a warning for any woman reading this. Please be careful about the men you bring into your life. There are still good Christian men out in the world. Be careful when you are dating someone who gives you a bad feeling because it just may be the Lord trying to tell you something. It took almost dying before my relative could see that young man for who he really was, and I hope her story might save someone else from that kind of pain.

Speaking of that young man, he still was not out of her life at this point. He was made even bolder since he had gotten away with what he had done, or perhaps he was always this way, but for whatever reason, he continued to contact my relative, even while she was healing from the attack. As soon as she blocked his phone number, he would find a way to contact her again, always trying to get her back as though nothing had happened. He still felt like he owned her body and soul, and he seemed baffled when she didn't want anything to do with him. When she did communicate with him, she kept all the messages and recorded the phone calls to keep as evidence.

Unfortunately, he did not stop at just messages and phone calls.

Once my relative was back in her own home, Deloris would visit with her and help her with her child. One evening, Deloris heard someone walking up into the yard. My relative's child, who was still quite small at the time, spotted who it was and said, "Uh, oh." Sure enough, it was him. When he saw Deloris standing out front, he made sure to keep his distance, especially after Deloris asked him, in a matter-of-fact way, "Do you want to get shot?" The young man did not miss a beat, however, explaining that he had gotten a ride from a friend and that he only wanted to talk. By this point, my relative had taken out a restraining order against him. Deloris reminded him of this and threatened to call the police. This ran him off, but Deloris and my relative were still shaken up by the experience.

Thankfully, things have died down a good deal since then regarding this stalking behavior. Still, she fears that the young man might try and return at any time, despite the restraining order.

I will not go into any more detail about that situation because my goal is not to identify anyone or slander anyone's name. I am telling you this to show you yet another example of how Satan has come against my family and how God prevailed and delivered us another miraculous hedge of protection. All praises to the heavenly Father for protecting her that day, for protecting her since, and for protecting my entire family.

***

One day in 2019, Deloris and I decided to go for a walk down the road in front of our home. We do not see too much traffic around here, so it is a safe route to take, and it gives us some fresh air and exercise. We had done this many times before, taking it easy, enjoying the sunshine, and talking about how far we have come in this life and where we are headed. Most of this walk is not too hard, but there is one small hill to climb. Any other time, we would have walked up it with no problems, but on that day, we were climbing the hill, and Deloris turned to me and said, "Hold me." We stood there for about fifteen minutes. At first, I thought she was only tired or dehydrated, but as we were walking back home, I could tell something wasn't quite right. She kept saying that she felt like her feet were in front of her body. Naturally, I wanted to take her to the hospital, even though she did not want me to make a fuss over her. We checked her blood pressure the next day, and the top number had shot up to over two hundred. I called one of my grandsons, who works in the medical field, and explained the situation to him. He told us to get her to the hospital immediately. In his professional opinion, he said it sounded like she had a stroke. In no time, we were at the hospital, where the doctor revealed to us that she had indeed suffered a stroke. They found blood concentrated all in the back of her head, inside her skull. The stroke affected her balance, gave her occasional problems with vertigo, and slightly affected her speech. Other than that, she felt fine.

We eventually had five doctors looking after her, and she was discharged within two days. They gave her some medicine that took care of the blood in her head, but she still gets dizzy when she walks too quickly. I am grateful that these are the only issues she has from her stroke because I have known people younger than her who have lost the use of their limbs from a stroke. Once again, the Great Physician was looking after my wife, just as He has looked after all of us so many times.

**

As if the stroke were not enough to deal with, the devil tried to get at Deloris once again a few years later. This time his attack was not health-related, though.

She was leaving the bank in her car, as she had done plenty of times before. Deloris is a careful driver. She never drives too fast, and she does not take any chances. She looked both ways, pulled out of the bank's parking lot, then a car slammed into the passenger's side of her car. Just as she realized what had happened, a man in a truck hit her head-on. The man kept on driving.

Thankfully, this was not a main road, so the impact of both these collisions was not nearly as intense as it could have been, although it's safe to say my wife was shaken up badly. The head-on impact had cracked the radiator in the car that had hit her, and steam seeped out from under the hood. At the moment, Deloris could not tell if the steam was coming from her own car or the other car, so she hopped out, thinking something was on fire. Miraculously, neither person was injured, and nothing caught fire. Deloris did not have a scratch on her. God reminded us that He was still in charge and that He was watching over us even during everyday tasks and trips. Remember, God does not just come to help us when we are in danger or up against incredible odds. He is also there when we do not even realize it, always guiding us, protecting us, and strengthening us on our walk with Him. People like to say it is a good thing to count your blessings. While it is never a bad idea to acknowledge what God has done in our lives, it is amazing to think about the things He's done for us without us even realizing it. Sometimes He pours out His blessings on us in ways we can clearly see, but do not forget that He is always blessing us, even if we cannot see it right then. When it comes to looking out for us, He never takes a day off, and He never gets tired. What a blessing it is!

A few years before this, the wife of one of my grandsons experienced her own vehicle-related incident. While driving behind another vehicle, she reached down into the floorboard of her car, looking for something. When she sat back up in her seat, she found that the car in front of her had stopped. She hit her brakes, but it was no use. Her car rolled five times from the impact. When I arrived at the scene of the wreck, my heart sank. Her car had ended up in a ditch, narrowly missing the water at the bottom of the ditch. It had rained the night before, and the water was several inches deep. If she had been knocked unconscious when she landed in the ditch, she could have drowned. The car itself looked like it had been through a warzone. Thankfully, no one was hurt, although she shared a humorous story that occurred just after the wreck.

She said that it had not taken long for several cars to pull off to the side of the road, either gawking at the wreck or trying to help. While she was lying in the ditch, shocked at what had happened and glad to be alive, a man got out of his car and approached her. "Don't move," he said quite seriously. "You're dead!" My grandson's wife did not know what to make of this. She only responded, "No. I'm not." The man said this a few more times before heading back to his car. You never know what kind of people you are going to meet in this life.

***

While I am talking about the times God has helped my family members, I want to stop for just a minute and talk more about Deloris' mother. This lady had always been a churchgoing, true woman of God, just as her husband was a man of God. She was never spiteful, hateful, or rude, but she did not let people walk all over her, either. She told you how she felt, and she rarely minced words.

Well, this led to me having a rocky relationship with my mother-in-law. When Deloris and I first married, I was not the man of God that I am now. God worked with me over the years to achieve that, but at that time, it caused some conflict between myself and Deloris' mother. We never had shouting matches or intense arguments, but I could tell she was trying to figure me out, and my reputation preceded me. I can't blame her at all.

Honestly, I would have felt the same way if I had been in her shoes. Thankfully, though, all that changed over time, and God saw fit for us to mend our relationship. Years later, Deloris' father passed away, and I began to hear that Deloris' mother was living on a tiny amount of money after her husband's death. Things got so bad for her that she had to put food back on the shelf at the grocery store because she could not afford it. Without delay, I decided that was going to change forever. I would do everything I could to take care of her financially. After following Christ all her life, it pained me to see her struggle in her golden years without anyone to lean on for help. She was my family member now, even if we had not agreed completely in the beginning.

At first, it was difficult since I was not bringing in much money, but I made it work. This was in the early 1990s when my company was just getting started. As God provided my company with increased work, I was able to financially help Deloris' mother more. She had a small home that she kept tidy and neat and rarely spent much money. She was grateful for my help, but money was not something she made a big fuss over. She paid her bills, bought food, and eventually purchased a modest car to help her get around town and hold onto her independence, which was a joy to see. Not once did she ever buy anything extravagant, and she never came to me wanting more money than I had given her that month. Some people would have taken that money, dressed in fancy clothes, gone out to expensive restaurants, and blown through it in no time, but she found much more joy in walking with her Savior. I was glad I had the honor of being in her life. In her later years, she gave me a card that read "Greatest Son-in-Law in the World." I still have that card today, and it makes me smile to think that I earned her respect and acceptance.

I continued to support my mother-in-law until her last day on this earth, but things were not always perfect for her. Through no fault of her own, she found herself in the devil's sights. Around 2018 or so, I was doing some work down along the Gulf Coast. Deloris had traveled with me down to the job site. It was good to have her with me, and it reminded me of when she and the kids came up to Washington State so many years ago to spend time with me out on the road. I have never shied away from demanding work, but it can sure get lonely when you're many hours away from your wife and family. I consider my employees as family members in a way, but it is just not the same, even when you enjoy working around so many good people.

We had planned to head back home for a while since the job would require many months of diligent work, but we ended up heading back a little earlier than planned. We did not realize it then, but God had sent us back at that particular time for an important task.

Unexpectedly, Deloris and I decided to visit her mother once we'd gotten back to Georgia. We were not even going to stop by our house first. I remember it was hot that day, the muggy, almost painful heat you experience in the Deep South during the middle of the summer. To make matters worse, there was not any breeze for miles. It was one of those days where neither of us missed having to drive vehicles with no air conditioning.

We arrived at Deloris' mother's home, and I parked my truck beside her car. Her mother was usually home most of the day, and it was normal for her to hear us pull into the driveway, peek out the front door, and come out front to greet us. On this day, however, we did not see her. We thought that she was inside watching television, cooking, or on the phone. I turned off my truck's ignition and opened the driver's side door, letting the first wave of humid South Georgia heat hit my skin. I started sweating as I walked up onto the front porch with Deloris right behind me, both of us squinting against the blazing sun until we found some relief under the shade of the front porch. I knocked and waited but heard nothing. I peeked through the glass, but I could not see any movement inside my mother-in-law's home.

Deloris and I looked at one another for a moment. Something did not add up.

We thought she was taking a midday nap, but that was not her usual routine. Maybe she had ridden off with a friend of hers to go to the grocery store. Glancing back at her car, it looked like it had not been moved in a while. Her home had a small back porch, but it was not enclosed or air-conditioned, so it would not have made sense for her to be out there in this kind of heat. Slowly, we stepped down off the front porch and checked the sides of the house. As we rounded the corner, we were not prepared for what we were about to see.

Out there in the blazing heat, Deloris' mother was lying in the grass just past the bottom step of her back porch. It looked like she had fallen as she was trying to climb the steps. It was clear that she had been there for some time—as much as a full day. She did not have a cell phone on her or a medical alert device, so we had no idea how long she had been there. We rushed to her side, expecting the worst. Thankfully, she opened her eyes and spoke to us in a weak, pitiful voice. We eased her upright as gently as we could but soon realized she had broken her hip. We could not take her in my truck without further injuring her, so we called the ambulance. The hospital treated her for severe dehydration and a nasty sunburn, but she recovered and was back to her old self in no time.

Had we decided to head straight home that day or to delay our trip back to Georgia, there is a good chance my mother-in-law would not have made it. She did not have any neighbors close by, so there is no telling how long it would have taken for someone to find her. Though we had no idea, God was working through us to protect Deloris' mother. I am glad He decided to send us to her that day. She was truly a special woman, and God decided it was not her time to come home quite yet. That was a few years later, and I was fortunate enough to be with her when God called her home.

In August of 2021, I went to see my mother-in-law. She was ninety-five years old at the time but had been in good health since breaking her hip a few years before. Something was different that day. She seemed unnaturally tired. Before long, she told me she was ready to go home to meet Jesus. To be clear, she was in her right mind, and she had never given any signs of Alzheimer's or dementia. Being the woman of God that she was and remembering what had happened with my grandmother on my dad's side of the family, I figured that God had given her a sign that the time had come. Immediately, I called Deloris and told her to come to her mother's home.

Deloris sat with her mother for a while, and they talked, sang, and spoke in tongues. We asked her if she was in any pain, and she assured us that she was not. We called up the ambulance, thinking it would be best to have her put in the hospital so the doctors could check her out, but she resisted the whole idea of going to the hospital. Still, we wanted to be sure we did all we could for her. The ambulance arrived, and the paramedic checked her vital signs. The paramedic looked at us and shook his head. "Her blood pressure is good," he said. The coronavirus was spreading through that area at that time, but he told us that she showed no signs of it. "I can't take her in the ambulance," he concluded, "because I can't find anything wrong with her. I can't force her to go." We thanked him for his time and his knowledge and wished him well as he left. Deloris and I understood that this was the way it had to be. We had done all we could to help, but when the time comes, there is nothing to do but be there with your loved one.

We stayed with my mother-in-law, praying, talking, and reminiscing. During one prayer, my mother-in-law spoke to her Savior, telling Him she was tired and ready to go home. After some time had passed, she asked Deloris for one of those meal replacement drinks that elderly people sometimes drink to help give them extra calories, protein, and vitamins. Of course, Deloris quickly brought the drink to her mother, and my mother-in-law drank it down in almost one gulp. This was unusual for her. She had never been a big woman, and she had eaten like a bird for most of her life. "Give me another one," she told Deloris. Just after she finished that second drink, she turned her head to the side as though she had fallen asleep. For just a moment, we thought she was only resting her eyes, but I noticed she was unnaturally still. To be sure, Deloris called my grandson, who works in the medical field. He instructed us to check her throat for signs of a pulse, but we did not find one. She did not suffer, and she was not scared at all. She was ready to go, and she had asked her Savior to take her home. For a child of God like my mother-in-law, death is not something to fear. Instead, it is a reward for your time being in the service of Almighty God. There is no doubt in my mind that she is with Christ. Her husband had liked to dance when he was young, so I imagine the two of them are dancing up in heaven right now.

After the funeral, Deloris and I went through her home, boxing up things and thinking back on all the memories her belongings brought up in our minds. To our surprise, we found some money stashed away here and there. As we kept going, we found more money. Before we were done, we discovered tens of thousands of dollars she had hidden away in drawers, cabinets, boxes, and such. I had been sending her money for all those years, and she had only spent what she needed to live after paying her bills and sending her tithes to the church. She could have easily bought herself so many wonderful things, but that just wasn't her style. By this point in the story, you know what a blessing it is for me to have met and married my wife, but I am so glad that I had the chance to have a woman like my mother-in-law in my life, as well. They say that when you marry a person, you marry their entire family, in a way. I have known people who have married a good person, but their in-laws have ruined their lives. I thank God that this was not the case for me. It really is a blessing to be with someone who comes from a family that walks with God.

***

We are coming to the end of my story, but I want to share with you a powerful event that happened to me. As it happened, this event revolved around my dad. I would never have thought it was possible, but he ended up giving me the opportunity to accomplish something I never thought I could do. For all his faults, he provided me with one of the greatest tests of my faith.

For years after he had killed my mother and grandmother, I had wrestled with the idea of forgiving him. What he did causes me pain to this day, but for many years it was too much to deal with. I would instead turn my attention to my work, my family, and my place in God's plan. As I grew in Christ, I realized that the Father had forgiven us all for so many things. I knew Christ had been beaten and had died for our transgressions. I wanted to be more like my heavenly Father, and I knew that to do that, I would eventually have to face my dad.

Many years after he had been in prison, I received word that he had cancer. There was not much time left, so I had to act quickly. I mustered up the strength to see him. Deloris went with me, supportive as always. She knew how important this was and how painful it would be, and she knew I would need her to lean on.

It took some time before they let me see my dad. I did not know what to expect since it had been years since I had seen his face. I was not sure how I would react. I was not ready yet. Maybe the memories of that horrible day would come rushing back, and I would leave without saying a word to him.

Instead, I found myself face-to-face with a man I barely recognized. I had always remembered him as being tough looking and stocky. I also remembered how strong he could be when he was in the middle of a drunken rampage. But the man in front of me that day was a shell of a man. His muscles were gone, and even his facial features were sunken. I knew he was sick, but I had not expected this.

For a long time, I had imagined what I would say to him if I ever saw him again. I had imagined what he would say to me. I had gone over it in my head at least a thousand times. I wanted closure. I needed some final word from him to end the pain in my heart, but he just sat there, barely even looking at me. I waited for him to speak, but he never did.

What was I feeling at that moment? Was it rage, pain, loss, or fear? At first, all those feelings swirled within me. Just as soon as those feelings crept up, though, a powerful sense of calm took over. So long ago, I was a helpless child at the mercy of his torment, and somewhere deep inside me, that little child was still alive in my soul, wondering why his dad had done all this. But now I was a man. No, I was more than that—I was a man of God, walking the path my Creator had laid out for me. I had suffered, I had failed, but I had also won so many great victories through the power and grace of the holiest God.

I looked at this man in front of me. I knew he was my dad, but at that moment, he had no power over me. This was the same man who had once told me, "You'll never amount to anything." That one phrase had replayed itself over and over a million times someplace deep in my mind, like a curse. But God had seen to it that those words my dad had spoken so long ago never came true. I was successful and blessed with a wonderful wife and wonderful children. When I was a child, I vowed to show my dad he was wrong, and I had done it.

At that moment, I looked at my dad in his withered state, and I forgave him. They were not just words, either. I forgave him in my heart and in my mind, just as my God had taught me to do. I waited for a time for my dad to reply, but he never did. Eventually, the guard took him away.

I left that place without hearing a word from my dad. For so long, I thought there was something he could say that would make it all make sense. I thought if I received any kind of closure, it would come from him. Instead, it came from my heavenly Father. My dad no longer held any power over me, and Satan could no longer use those events of my past to attack my mind and work against God's plan. Though losing my mother and grandmother still causes me great pain, God continues to lighten that burden each day. As angry as I was at my dad, it helps me to know that he accepted Jesus as his savior while in prison. Despite everything that happened, he was my dad, and I loved him. One day I will see him again in glory, and we will not have that pain to divide us any longer. We will simply be children of God. I look forward to seeing him again.

Chapter 9

Now this story comes full circle. You have seen how our heavenly Father has, time again, protected me from the barbs and snares of Satan, as well as my own personal flaws and shortcomings. You have witnessed how our Father has made a way for me, just as the old hymn says He will make a way when there seems to be no way. Even when I doubted myself, He had a plan, and He never once doubted me or gave up on me. You have also seen how Satan has tried to get to me indirectly by attacking my friends and family members through the years and how he has personally attacked me. Once again, God was there, watching over all of us.

Today, I live a peaceful life. I thank the Father every day for His blessings on myself and my family and for allowing me to live this long in such good health so that I can enjoy His many wonderful blessings and continue to do His will as He has instructed me. I still donate to the International Fellowship of Christians and Jews, and I am glad to say that, as of this writing, I am not only helping them to achieve aliyah by returning them to the holy land, but I am also helping to feed and clothe them. It is my goal to eventually provide housing for them and much more. It gives me such joy to help God's chosen people, and I am so thankful that He entrusted me with doing this. It helps to give me a purpose and a drive to continue operating my thriving company when some people in my situation would simply keep making money and buying things they do not really need. That is not to say that I do not purchase some nice things here and there for myself, my wife, or my friends and family, but I've come to realize that two of the most fulfilling things in this world are time spent with good people and helping good people. Giving back energizes me, and you could say that it has become a mission of mine during this time of my life. From time to time, Deloris and I have given to certain members of our little community and to organizations that share our goal of truly helping others. We enjoy seeing the positive change this makes in people's lives, and that makes all the difference. Most of this is done anonymously since it has never been about us. Instead, we see ourselves as simply answering God's call to be His helping hands on this earth. He is given so much to us that it would be selfish not to give back. All this success is His anyway because none of it would have been possible without Him. When it comes down to it, our very survival is because of Him, as I have shown you our brushes with death over the years.

This small town where I live hasn't changed much since I first decided to put down roots here, and I like that. Life hums along at an easy pace. Sometimes, when I am walking across the bridge I have built out over the pond behind my house, I think back to all the events of my life. I think about the bitter cold of Alaska when I was so desperate to make money so I could provide for my family in our time of need. I think of my travels in the Navy and the wide-open ocean. I think of all the good people who have helped me over the years or taken a chance on me since there is really no such thing as a truly self-made man—everybody needs someone along the way. I think about my wonderful wife, who has been there for me when other women might have given up on me or wanted a different kind of life.

Now that I have entered my eighth decade of being on this earth, I am becoming much more aware of how short our lives are and how precious our time is here. God has seen fit to keep me in excellent health even at my age, and He gives me the mental clarity and energy to stay in decent shape, so I can continue to do His work and enjoy my life when so many others my age are beginning to lose their quality of life to illnesses, broken bones, and decreased energy. Unfortunately, many of my friends and acquaintances did not get to see their eightieth birthdays. I have lived through the grief of so many leaving this world, but knowing they were children of God soothes my sadness. This world is not all there is, and only through Christ can we live forever in heaven. I think about the friends and family members who are no longer here with me: my mother, my grandmother, Deloris' parents, my friend Jack, and so many others. As hard as it might be for you to believe, I still think of my dad from time to time. Regardless of what he did in this life, I do not think he was an evil man. There were times when I hated him. I'm only human. But as hard as it was to forgive him for taking my mother and grandmother from me, I did it because Christ first forgave me.

All the people who have passed away now live on in my memories. As sad as it may be to think about them, I smile when I think of what a happy day it will be when we're all reunited, walking the streets of glory together as one big family, safe with the Father in a place where there is no more pain, no more loss, and nothing to worry about ever again. Oh, what a day that will be! All the problems of this life will fall away, and we will be with the Father at last.

I know I can look forward to that blessed day. I know God is real. I know His Son, Jesus Christ, died for all of us on the cross at Calvary, and I know the Holy Spirit is real. If there was ever any doubt in my mind, the events of my life have shown me otherwise. I don't know why, but God the Father decided to work with me, show me His power, and set me on the path He ordained for me. When He keeps revealing His love and grace to you over and over, you cannot help but take notice and understand what is happening.

But that has been my experience. It was easy for me to recognize His work in my life since it has always been so clear and obvious. Your life might be quite different from mine, but I hope you will recognize the work of the Father in your life just as you have seen His work in mine.

The whole point of this book is to share what He has done for me. I sleep soundly, knowing there is a place for me in glory. Maybe you are already a believer and have given your life to Christ. If that is the case, I ask you to use this story to strengthen your faith and to never forget that God loves you and is always there for you, even if it sometimes seems like you are all alone in this world. If you're not already a believer, I hope my life's story will show you that God is real and that He loves you. Honestly, I have no idea why He chose to work with me the way

He has. I'm not a saint, a prophet, or anything special, really. That is the thing about Him—He knows everything about you, the good and the bad, and He loves you just the same. If you're not a believer, you might think I'm simply crazy. You might think I am making all this up. I can assure you, dear reader, that all of what you have read is the truth. I have left out the names of some folks or changed some names to protect the identities of certain people, but the events happened just as they are described in this book. If you have not given your life to Christ and you have gotten this far in my story, it might be that there is something within you compelling you to keep reading. The Father is trying to communicate with you since He has many ways of doing that. If that is the case, I want to ask you to accept Him into your heart. Now, I cannot force you to make that decision—I would not even if I could. God Himself does not force us to believe. He gives all of us a choice. All I know is that life is amazing once you've given your heart over to Jesus. Things will not be perfect, but there is a peace that comes with it. The Scriptures call it a peace that "surpasses all understanding," and that sounds exactly right to me. I experience it every day. If you have never given your life to Christ, I simply ask that you consider doing so because I would like for you to enjoy that peace, as well. I cannot promise that God will work the kinds of miracles in your life that He has in mine, but I know that your life will be better in ways you cannot yet imagine. It does not matter where you come from. It does not matter what kind of pain and suffering you have endured or may be living through as you read this. You might feel like you are broken, helpless, worthless, and have no reason to live. If that is the case, I want you to find comfort in our Almighty God. To Him, you are wonderful. You are a unique, beautiful, priceless treasure deserving of His divine love.

Throughout my life, I have tried to make myself more like Him, even though that is impossible to accomplish fully. He has given me so much over the years and continues to pour out His blessings on me. Yes, I donate to many charities, individuals, and organizations, but if you are not yet a believer, I want to extend to you the greatest thing I can give. I know His love for me and for all of us, and I want you to have that, too, because that is the greatest gift I can help you achieve. His love goes far beyond money, fame, or any material possession. But I cannot do it for you. You must profess your belief in Christ and accept Him into your heart. I hope you do so, my friend, so that He can bless your life and so I can one day see you in glory. As wonderful as God has been to me over the course of my life, I do not want to be selfish with these blessings. Again, they came from Him, so I cannot take credit for them. I want to bless others, and the most important way for me to do that is to help lead others to Christ. If just one person reading this accepts Christ as his or her Savior, then my life will have been worth living. May the Father receive all the glory for anything good I have done in this life and anything I may do before my days are through.

Today I enjoy much more peace and security than I ever did before. I find spiritual security in knowing I am on the path God has laid out for me, knowing without a doubt that I am doing His will for His glory. I have financial security beyond anything I could have ever imagined when I was a child. This is only because of the blessings of my Creator, who placed me in the situations I needed to be in and gave me the knowledge and willpower to achieve that financial security. I enjoy the security of having my loving wife here with me and my family and friends near and far. We have all been through so much, and there will surely be more trials and tribulations ahead. Even so, I know we will never be without the grace, mercy, protection, and love of the Father.

My children have long since moved out, so it is just Deloris and myself here at our home, although friends and family often stop by to visit, and we certainly enjoy their company. Some people might find that a lonely existence, but we are never really alone. The Father is here with us, always. For many years, I have made it a point to keep my home a welcome place for Him. I spend my mornings exercising, then spending time in my prayer closet, where I talk with Him, thank Him, and pray for His protection over my family and all the people I know. It took many years of waiting, patiently listening for that still, small voice to direct me toward whatever it was He wanted me to do. Even now, I still listen. I keep my antenna up because if you do not listen, you will not hear.

Not too long ago, after I had been donating to help Jews around the world, He spoke to me just as He did when He commanded me to bring His people home. I was at home in my prayer closet, giving Him my undivided time for that portion of the day. Out of nowhere, He said, "You have touched My heart for the love of My people." After all, I have been through, after all the ups and downs, the victories and defeats, to hear that from the Father Himself was just about enough to bring me to tears. Knowing I had done what He commanded and that I was still doing what He wanted, filled me with an almost unspeakable joy. But that was not all. He continued by saying, "I have blessed you in the past, but the best is yet to come." Naturally, I do not worry too much about what that might be because He has it all under control. I have to say, though, that I am more than a little curious. He will accomplish His will when the time is right for Him—no sooner, no later. I suspect that the "best" that is "yet to come" might have something to do with this book, or it might be something you do because you read this book. It will reach those who need to hear this story. It will help someone. That is all I can ask for, really. This book is not about my glorification. Instead, it is about lifting up my Almighty Father and telling others about the love, grace, mercy, and amazing blessings He has seen fit to bestow on me.

I am grateful for all His blessings. I'm a simple person when it comes down to it. I find joy in working in my company and seeing it benefit the lives of all my employees and their families, as well. I enjoy going out to eat, as well as drinking a cup of coffee in the morning with my dear, sweet wife. I enjoy staying connected with friends and family, helping people in my community, the feel of the steering wheel of my favorite truck when I hit the road, and the quiet, peaceful life I live.

Sometimes I watch the news, and it makes me a little upset at the way the world is headed. I cannot do anything to change the course of history, but I can be of service to my Father and my fellow human beings while I'm here. I am certain the Father has more in store for me. He's given me a job to do, and I am going to do it to the best of my ability for as long as I can. Even so, I look forward to the day when I can see His face, touch the hem of His garment, and hear Him say, "Well done, my good and faithful servant." I pray that you'll be there too, dear reader, and we can rejoice together in the presence of the Father. Until then, I will continue to serve Him, and I will always share the story of how He's worked miracles in my life, though I did not deserve any of it. If He has done all this for me, what will He do for you? All you must do is trust in Him and give your life over to Him.

When I was a young boy, my world was a place of chaos most of the time. As I grew older, the challenging work it took to provide for myself and my family was another kind of chaos, although I'd do it all over again for my family. Today, my life is one of peace. It is nice and quiet out here where I live. Few people ever drive by my house, and those who do are usually either my neighbors or folks I know personally. Sometimes I just look out at the pond, my yard, my home, and my vehicles and thank God that this is where I have ended up. I could not have asked for a better life. Deloris and I still eat most of our meals together, and we are still just as in love and committed to one another as when we first got married. That is one of the greatest blessings of my life since most people are not fortunate enough to stay together with the same person for sixty years or more. What makes it even better is that she is someone I have wanted to be with for every one of those sixty years, and she feels the same about me. Whatever comes along, I know I can handle it with the help of the Father and with a true woman of God like Deloris by my side. She has always been there for me, even when I might not have believed in myself.

My life could have turned out in so many other ways. I could have never met Deloris. I could have ignored God's call. I could have slipped into alcoholism or drug use, as so many good people have been lost to those horrible snares of Satan. I could have died in the Navy or been injured or killed on those tough jobs in Alaska. I might never have found that work in Alaska at all and let my family down. It hurts me to think of all the ways my life could have turned out, but I thank God the Father that He decided to lead me here, to this place, with all these wonderful people in my life, with a successful company, and a home filled with love where God is always welcome.

Yes, I can honestly say I've been blessed.

Epilogue

I am almost eighty and a half years old, and Deloris is seventy-nine. We both hope that whoever reads about the wonderful things God has done for us will also experience the same things as they trust God to reveal His perfect plan for their lives. To know experientially what it means to be kept by the power of God is like a dream come true. Like I have said before, I am nobody special, but because He loved me and I was willing to submit to His Lordship, He saved me and transformed me into one of His many servants who strive to know and do His will.

As I continue to do God's will, I know the adversary, that diabolical spirit, will continue to war against me and anyone who knows God and desires to keep His commandments. Also, the devil will continue to work through those who do not know God.

My family and I would like to thank God again for pushing back the schemes of the devil before he could render us powerless. We acknowledge that we are overcomers because of His Spirit, which lives within our hearts, and believe, as the Bible says, "Greater is he that is in you, than he that is in the world" (1 John 4:4, KJV).

Recently, the schemes our adversary presented to us would occur after Deloris and I went for a walk. Suddenly, she fell forward, and I was not able to catch her. I called an ambulance, and they took her to Wayne Memorial in Jesup, Georgia. She would have been airlifted by helicopter and flown to Savannah Memorial, but the weather prevented this, and the pilot canceled the flight on July 18th, 2022. At first, the prognosis was not good because she was unconscious for the first week, and there was little evidence of her ever awakening again. Even two of my family members felt this was it and that she would soon depart from this life. But because God's people joined in prayer, wonderful things began to take place. Deloris was on a journey of gradually returning to her prior condition before the stroke. It was as if God was letting us know; He had heard our prayers and would answer each one of them.

She remained at Savannah Memorial for three weeks before transferring to a rehabilitation facility in Jacksonville, Florida, on August 7th, 2022. In a couple of days, she was walking down the hallway with a walker and did not require any help from the nurses who walked beside her. She successfully exercised and continued to regain her strength.

Deloris is scheduled to remain at the rehabilitation facility until September 15th, 2022.

As I reflect on all the trials and tribulations that have affected my family and me, I do not think I will ever cease to be amazed at how He has always intervened the entire time. His promises are to all who believe. He said, "I will never leave nor forsake you."

At this time in my life, I am at peace and content to always strive to obey God and thank Him for the day He prompted my sister-in-law by His Spirit to inform me to record the events that have transpired throughout my brief life. After hearing this, the next night, while I was lying on my bed, He confirmed to me that I was to author this book.

I accomplished this task because God said, "No!"